What Readers and Critics say about the Poetry of Felix Dennis

"Felix Dennis is the real thing — a genuine poet who combines feeling, image and linguistic delicacy with his own kind of energy and honesty. I love reading his verse and you will too."
   — **Stephen Fry,** *actor, writer and director*

"This is marvellous stuff... a 21st century Kipling. He rollicks and rolls with rhyme, meter, and melody."
   — **Tom Wolfe,** *critic and author*

"He writes like a man obsessed… If Waugh were still alive, he would fall on Dennis's verse with a glad cry of recognition and approval."
   — **John Walsh,** *The Independent*

"It is so rare one comes across a modern poet whose talent leaps off of every page and who has had the good grace to respect poetry by using rhyme, paying attention to cadence, and, at the same time, so involving you in each poem, you forget these necessary structures. Not since the Welsh poet-magician, Dylan Thomas, has a British poet seemed so well poised to gain a wide audience…"
   — **Alan Caruba,** *Editor, bookviews.com*

"Normally, I only pretend to like poetry, but with Felix's stuff I hardly have to pretend at all. Annoyingly good."
   — **Hugh Grant,** *actor*

"I enjoy his poetry immensely."
   — **Mick Jagger,** *singer, songwriter*

"Great quality and memorability. At least one of these poems will be instantly anthologised."
   — **Melvyn Bragg,** *broadcaster and author*

"...an engaging monster, filled with contradictions and reeking of sulphur."
   — *The Times*

"Felix Dennis has done a restoration job on the state of poetry in this country. As with Pablo Neruda, he has that simple ability to throw language like a dress over experience, and make the mundane marvellous. In an age when poets have forgotten how to sing, or scorn to do so, he sings like the Heavenly Muse."
   — **Christopher Rush,** *author*

"What a total, utter joy to receive a copy of Felix Dennis's latest collection of poetry… almost guaranteed to be one of the biggest-selling books of new poetry in the UK. He gives us a volume packed with unpretentious poems drawn largely from his own life, experiences and observations — this is what makes them so real, so readable and, above all, so enjoyable."
   — **Richard Fair,** *bbc.co.uk*

"I don't know which is better: hearing [him] read them aloud or reading the book itself. Deftly amusing on first hearing, his verse repays much closer inspection."
   — **Dotun Adebayo,** *BBC Radio London*

"*A Glass Half Full* is the poetry of real life… the power to raise a smile in one who never laughs; to wring tears from another who hasn't wept since kindergarten; and to bring a measure of consolation to the inconsolable."
   — **Anita Lafford**, *sculptor*

"An unforgettable evening… to hear him perform was awe-inspiring."
   — **Sandy Holt**,
   The Stratford-upon-Avon Herald

"*A Glass Half Full* is funny, poignant and a breath of fresh air."
   — **Sarah Broadhurst**, *The Bookseller*

"Dennis confronts issues ranging from the holocaust to Elvis with equal poetic and emotional skill. The verse sweeps from darkly poignant to hilariously funny."
   — **John Severs**,
   Ottakar's New Title Reviews

"Dennis is a crouching tiger about to wreak mayhem amongst the bleating lambs of English poetry."
   — **Mick Farren**, *novelist and poet*

"A knockout! Full of wisdom, compassion, humour and worldly insight."
   — **Richard Neville**, *author and broadcaster*

"Serious, witty, thought provoking and moving. You may even cry! I loved it."
   — **Dave Reynolds**, *Radio Warwick*

"One can recreate the visual image so clearly— hearing, sense of touch, sense of smell— they are so evocative in his poetry. It's enthralling."
   — **Isobel Yule**,
   National Library for the Blind and RNIB

"I did not go gently into that dark room, but within minutes I knew that we were in the company of talent… at once wise and maddeningly childish, optimistic and grim."
   — **Dawn French**, *actor and comedienne*

"Many people were deeply moved by the humanity of his verse and by the range of his experience [in these] haunting poems."
   — **Tom Wujec**, *TED (Technology, Entertainment &Design) Conference, Monterey, California*

"I don't think I have ever known such a sense of celebration and occasion in all of the years of our poetry programme. You feel he lived it so richly, so dangerously, so that he could be so wise for our delight"
   — **Dr. Robert Woof**,
   Director of The Wordsworth Trust, scholar and author

"Sometimes moving, sometimes amusing, his words are beautifully crafted, accessible, fascinating and unforgettable. To watch him performing is pure magic."
   — **Clare Fitzsimmons**, *Stratford Observer*

"I enjoyed *A Glass Half Full* more than I can possibly say. Brilliant!"
— **Helen Gurley Brown,**
Editor in Chief, Cosmopolitan

"Dennis is a literary star in his own right. He makes it look easy— damn him! I couldn't put the book down. Just one question remains: what took Dennis so long to come out as a poet? And are there more where these came from? God, I hope so!"
— **Z. Menthos,** *critic.org*

"A fantastic collection! Rich, sumptuous and beautifully threaded."
— **Jon Snow,** *Channel 4 broadcaster*

"The way poetry should be. The sort of book that can make poetry popular again."
— **Alex Frankel,** *amazon.co.uk*

"A one of a kind book. Some poems [are] delicious, deeply sensitive and serious; others [are] humorous, even bawdy. For poetry lovers with a liking for dry humor and much wit… I highly recommend it. Five stars."
— **Elizabeth R. Mastin,** *amazon.com*

"His poetry is like cappuccino— a light frothy top conceals a dark strong flavour. Startlingly humorous with profound observations on life."
— **Ron Westrich,**
The Stratford-upon-Avon Herald

"Those of you who missed Felix Dennis at his UK-wide tour appearances should weep. By the fourth poem he had the audience drinking out of his hand."
— **Don Barnard,** *Reviews Gate.com*

"Felix Dennis is a poet of the Hemingway, Kipling, Frost or even Rod McKuen variety… It will not take long for the world to realize his genius and voice. His poetry is that good."
— **Claudia VanLydegraf,** *myshelf.com*

"I was enticed along to an evening of Felix Dennis's poetry by the promise of free wine, but in all honesty I would happily pay to see him again and again! If all poetry was written with the same passion, humour and sense of nostalgia and morality as this, then poetry would once again be one of the foremost art forms in this country."
— **Martin G. Bryant,** *amazon.co.uk*

"*A Glass Half Full* contains the best poetry in decades."
— **Jed Pressgrove,** *The Reflector, College Publisher Network*

"Felix Dennis gives us poetry with roots in the 60s and a 21st century relevance. I could rave on, but I won't. Get your own copy and settle down with a glass of vino— you have hours of enjoyment ahead."
— **Hilary Williamson,** *bookloons.com*

Homeless in My Heart

Homeless in My Heart

Felix Dennis

Designed by Rebecca Jezzard

Photographs supplied from the archives of
Science Photo Library and National Geographic Society

EBURY
PRESS

By the Same Author

A Glass Half Full
(Hutchinson) 2002

Lone Wolf
(Hutchinson) 2004

The Taking of Saddam:
A Ballad
(Noctua Press) 2004

When Jack Sued Jill:
Nursery Rhymes for Modern Times
(Ebury Press) 2006

Island Of Dreams:
99 Poems from Mustique
(Noctua Press) 2007

EBURY
PRESS

Set in Sabon and Univers

All titles are available from good booksellers.

www.felixdennis.com
contains many poems, published and unpublished,
as well as a library of sound recordings and video footage
of Felix Dennis's verse and poetry tours.

1 3 5 7 9 10 8 6 4 2

Published in 2008 by Ebury Press, an imprint of Ebury Publishing

A Random House Group Company

The Random House Group Limited Reg. No. 954009

Addresses for companies within the Random House Group can be found at
www.randomhouse.co.uk

A CIP catalogue record for this book is available from the British Library

Printed and bound in the UK by Butler, Tanner & Dennis Ltd

ISBN 9780091928001

To buy books by your favourite authors and register for offers visit www.rbooks.co.uk

Every effort has been made to contact and clear permissions with relevant copyright holders.

Photographs courtesy of Science Photo Library

National Geographic images:
George Steinmetz for the photograph on page 114
David Doubilet for the image on page 122
Jack Newton for the photograph on page 193
Mark Thiessen for the photograph on page 198
Tom Abel (SLAC, Stanford University) and Ralf Kaehler (SLAC, Stanford University) for the computer simulation on page 216

The 105 poems in *Homeless in My Heart* were written between 2004 and early 2008. Sixteen of them have appeared previously in *Island of Dreams* and one in *Clouds In My Coffee*. To view many that have not been published, as well as those already in print, go to **www.felixdennis.com**

For Don Atyeo

You were better than ever you knew;
In motley, you were peerless.
When the bells of a jester ring true,
They are lordly — and fearless.

— 'The Wise Fool'

Preface

My mind cries out to startled hands:
'Tear up his map, his chart!
This creature of a thousand lands
Is homeless in his heart.'

'Home is where you come to when you have nothing better to do.'

So Margaret Thatcher told *Vanity Fair* in 1991, though I doubt there were too many occasions on which such a woman had 'nothing better to do'.

Robert Frost, in 'The Death of the Hired Man', suggested:

> *Home is the place where, when you have to go there,*
> *They have to take you in.*

But that presupposes someone else present to make such a decision. Cannot a person who lives alone claim to have a 'home'?

My favourite modern quotation on the subject comes from Christopher Fry in 'The Lady's not for Burning':

> *The best*
> *Thing we can do is make wherever we're lost in*
> *Look as much like home as we can.*

Philip Larkin's 'Home is so Sad' is a close runner-up:

> *Home is so sad. It stays as it was left,*
> *Shaped to the comfort of the last to go*
> *As if to win them back.*

So what is 'home'? The most comforting word in any language? A place of refuge? A room where you hang your hat? A roof to keep the rain off? A fortress? Somewhere we feel comfortable enough to strip off those masks we present to the outside world? A status symbol? The most expensive thing most of us will ever buy? The centre of our emotional (or, at least, our domestic) gravity?

'Home' is probably all these things. And, for some, a great deal more. But whatever and wherever it is, I know that I have never truly made one for myself.

Despite five residences scattered around the world, there is not a single one of them unavailable for my friends to stay in. Nor have I ever cared who uses my bed if I am absent. It has always been so for me. As Marianne Moore so aptly put it in her poem 'Silence' (through the mouth of her father) in a line appropriated from Edmund Burke:

> Nor *was he insincere in saying, "Make my house your inn."*
> *Inns are not residences.*

For me, my residences are places to eat and sleep in, to work in, to relax and entertain in, to share with friends. But they are not 'homes'. It took me a long time to realise this.

Today, perhaps, through writing and studying poetry, and from a late interest in the consolations of philosophy, I have begun to discover why this should be. Just as I love to act the fool, but am not a foolish man; as I enjoy throwing parties, but remain a solitary individual; and as I look forward to performing on stage, although I abhor crowds, so my love affair with a variety of bolt-holes, lairs and retreats is the antithesis of the usual concept of 'home'.

I believe my true home is in my mind. I remember mentioning this one evening to a close friend who eyed me narrowly over the top of his whisky glass and glanced pointedly about him: 'Must get pretty lonely in there,' he said, 'seeing as we are only ever invited into the foyer.'

It was a fair comment, although I have worked hard in recent years through my poetry to begin opening a few doors beyond that 'foyer'— both for my own sake and for any who might wish to accompany me. What I found there has formed the basis for many of the poems in this and my other books of verse.

To use Christopher Fry's terminology, I am making wherever I am look as much like home as I can. It is the best that I can do.

And the best, I strongly suspect, that many of us can do.

> — **Felix Dennis**
> *Soho, London 2008*

In the Dark

I knuckle an eye with my fist—
   Fragments of non-existent light
Erupt where they cannot exist,
   Blinding my non-existent sight.

We huddle by day in our joys,
   Swaddled in rags of silk and hope
Like toddlers at play with toys:
   By night, we twist all silk to rope

To tether the tiger, Desire,
   And cradle demons, lest they wake
And set the lakes of Guilt afire,
   As the walls of our dreaming shake.

The candle has guttered and died.
   Here in the dark— within my mind
My terrors and tigers collide:
   And all have eyes, but I am blind.

WEST INDIES, 2006

Aurora Borealis over coniferous forest, Canada.

'I do not know who made me...'

I do not know who made me,
Still less do I care,
The sheep that dot the meadow
Make no altar there.

Of transubstantiation
Beetles never learn,
The foxes build no bonfires
Where heretics must burn.

2

The bees that gather honey
Propagate in sin,
Nor do they slay in *jihad*
Their unbelieving kin.

No missionary weasels
Slither on the sly,
Nor does the dormouse tell me
That I must kneel or die.

Your words are your opinions,
Who knows what is true?
I do not know who made me—
And neither, friend, do you.

WARWICKSHIRE, 2006

'The world would be astonished if it knew how great a proportion of its brightest ornaments, of those most distinguished even in popular estimation for wisdom and virtue, are complete sceptics in religion.'
— **John Stuart Mill (1806 - 1873)**, English essayist and philosopher, who quite certainly included himself in such a 'proportion'.

Marigold pollen grain.

Wool and synthetic fibres.

That's the Truth

'That's the truth.' And yet it's not.
Part invention, part forgot,
Part embroidered by the weaver—
Memory, that warped deceiver,
Spinning, spinning in our head
Yarns of non-existent thread.

Tasselled falsehoods: 'You were king.'
We know we were no such thing:
Fabricated recollection
Loops the truth with false perception,
Spinning, spinning joy and wrath,
On a non-existent cloth.

LONDON, 2006

5

Sodium chloride, Salt.

On Attending a Reunion

I should not have come here, I knew that I shouldn't;
The past has been cast in the present's contempt;
I'd sworn to myself, I had sworn that I wouldn't;
The tide has washed over the dreams that we dreamt.

The lanterns that burn in the stern of our vessel
Light only the wrecks of survivors marooned;
I should not have come here— the mortar and pestle
Of time has been grinding its salt in the wound.

Old memories harboured in fond recollection
Lie shattered and ship-wrecked; I should not have come;
Better the rose-tinted seas of reflection,
Better the mermaids of youth should be dumb.

WARWICKSHIRE, 2004

Migrant Memories

In spring, I soak the verge outside my gate;
    My neighbours think me lunatic— or bored —
As seated on a stile, I watch and wait:
    A flash of acrobatics my reward.

The smaller things in life loom larger now.
    If once I courted wealth with sword and blood,
My pirate boots today can play the plough
    For swooping migrants scooping up the mud.

And while I watch their joyous, plunging flight,
    I contemplate the years of brag and theft,
The dreary, squalid years when might made right,
    This mercenary bounty all that's left.

    The air is filled with wings, yet strangely calm:
    'The best that men can do, is do least harm.'

WARWICKSHIRE, 2005

8

How many others, I wonder, watch and wait for the return of 'their' house martins and swallows each year? And how do such tiny birds make that immense annual journey, braving the firepower of idiotic Mediterranean 'marksmen' and the ravages of wind and storm, to re-build their mud nests in the same eaves? Two years ago, a house martin chick fell from one of the nests around my home onto the grass. Before replacing it, I attached a tiny red plastic band around one of its legs. Sure enough, the same bird has made the journey to Africa and back twice now, and is busy rearing yet another clutch of chicks outside my window as I type this.

Dried mud.

Volcanic eruption.

'We knew immediately...'

We knew immediately. A wide-eyed look...
I searched your eyes and knew what was in mine:
An invitation we must both decline—
But as you sipped your wine your fingers shook,
And mine shook, too. Vesuvius erupts!
I gabbled as I fought the urge to tear
The silk from off your back and do it there,
While fainting matrons gloated in their cups.
But we are neither young, nor cruel, and so—
The moment passed, or rather, we forsook
What in our youth would not have seemed so mad
As it seems now; world's shame we never took
The rightful path of easing such a blow:
And if we had — might that have been so bad?

WARWICKSHIRE, 2008

Slice of agate, a form of quartz.

'Grief seeks Loss...'

Grief seeks Loss —
    and moves in, uninvited,
Maggot-like,
    it hollows out a core;
Dipped in Guilt
    a sepulchre is whited,
Filled with Pain
    a residence is built;
Bricked with Fear
    and shuttered up with hating,
Dark and drear
    the empty rooms above,
Sealed within,
    Grief settles down to waiting;
Late, so late!
    arrives the bailiff, Love.

13

WEST INDIES, 2006

The coat of a fox

'I have paid more for a kiss…'

I have paid more for a kiss than a kiss
And that was error, sure—
Sucking on chemical bliss
In the tattooed arms of a store-bought whore.
You may blame me, certainly, if you wish—
And might as well blame a bear
For dining on silver fish,
Or a fox for stalking an old brown hare.

Those who pay more for a kiss than a kiss,
They pay with their lives, no less—
Swallow your hypocrite hiss:
The lost have need of a soft caress.
You may blame us, certainly, should you care,
Pelt us with stones and rocks,
But nothing will stay the bear,
Or spare a hare from a hungry fox.

WARWICKSHIRE, 2006

'And learn that the best thing is
To change my loves while dancing
And pay but a kiss for a kiss'
 — **W.B.** Yeats 'The Collarbone of a Hare'*

*By permission of A P Watt Ltd on behalf of Gráinne Yeats

A Sonnet of Useless Advice to a Young 'Un

Try to be brave— but not too brave, or swift,
   Learn from the birch and bow before the blast,
   The oaks are proud until the storm is passed,
Their stately limbs half-shattered and adrift.

Try to be true— but know that truth is masked,
   And each man's truth is his, and his alone;
   A friend may be more true than flesh and bone,
Yet hesitate to render truth, unasked.

Try to be kind— but keep yourself from those
   Whom you judge fools, or charlatans, or mad.
   Nor should you play the part of Galahad
Unless you seek your recompense in blows.

   Try to be wise— but hide your wisdom well:
   The world reveres a pearl, but not its shell.

WARWICKSHIRE, 2005

Interior view of an abalone shell, mother of pearl.

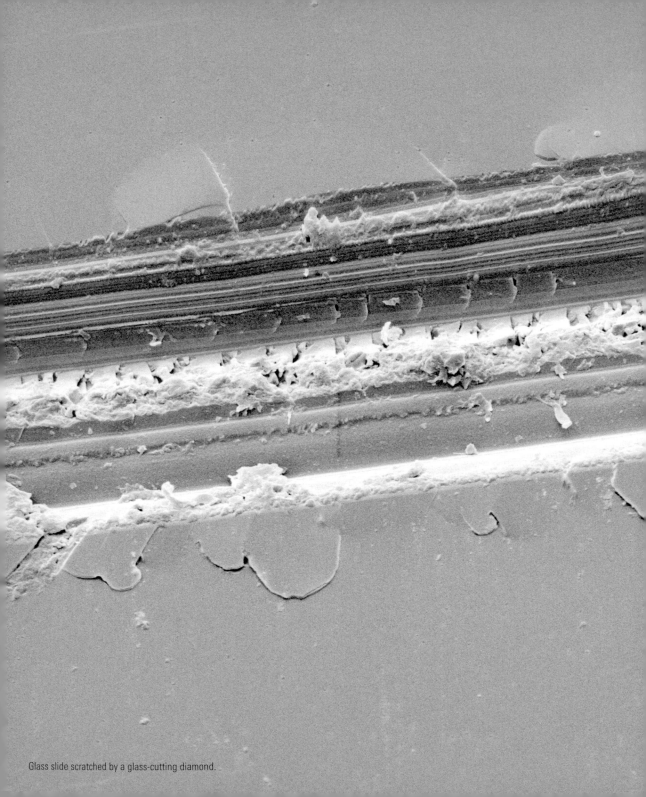

Glass slide scratched by a glass-cutting diamond.

Wars on Rome
(To a Sulking Child)

What wars on Rome were ever acts of sense?
The dead of Carthage lie beneath the clay —
Defiance is no proxy for defence,
Nor tears the coin of mercenaries' pay.

As Men look back, they see through prismed glass
Where what they think they know is warped by writ,
A victor's gloss on what has come to pass,
Each shade of grey consigned to line the pit.

You war on me — and yet I shall not war.
Your infant rage may harden into spite,
Yet I have faced such feeble rage before
And lived to tell the tale. Might makes all right.

Not fair? Not *fair*? Aye, nor was Rome to Greece.
The world was never fair: now make your peace.

WARWICKSHIRE, 2008

Eroded rock walls at Antelope Canyon, Arizona.

'I just stepped out...'

Where am I? — Oh, I just stepped out,
No need to make a fuss, or shout,
No need to comb the nearest wood
Or roam about the neighbourhood.

Call off the dog— she'll find no scent,
Please don't worry where I went,
And do not climb the garden tree,
My dear, you'll catch no glimpse of me.

The attic steps will pinch your thumb,
The cellar will be dark and dumb,
Yet should you search your heart with care,
Though I am gone, you'll find me there.

LONDON, 2007

Quitclaim

Of what should we be made except the past?
Just as the Earth is two thirds salt-rimed sea
And one third metalled rock, so history
Betrays the mould in which all things were cast.

The pot outlives the potter, and at last
Outlives the very wheel that spun it free;
Hauled from a wreck, a blank-faced refugee
Of skills long since forgotten or surpassed.

The pot is still a pot— it's worldly fate
Now severed from its maker's hand and name,
As each of us is free to shed the weight
Guilt wound about our cot with threads of blame.

    The past is what has made us, yet no womb
    Retains a claim beyond the catacomb.

WARWICKSHIRE, 2007

22

Quitclaim (noun & verb) a formal
renunciation of any claim against
obligation, person or property.

Alligator River Delta in Kakadu National Park, Northern Australia.

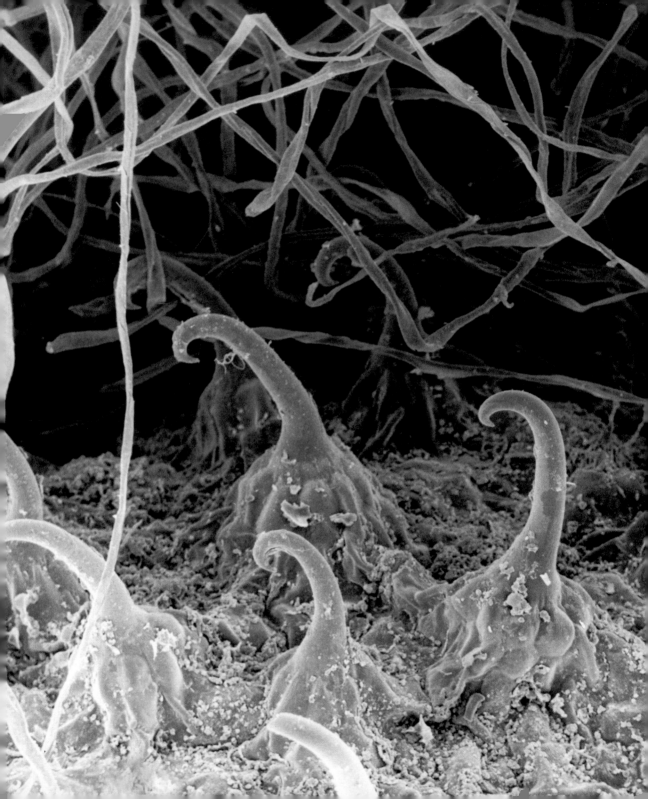

All Nature's Art

All Nature's Art is purest accident,
Not in or of itself— how should she know?—
But in the quality of what is lent
By those who view what Providence made so.

Take grass of softest green— in beetles' eyes
A dreary, harsh savanna, spiked and bound
In monochrome and perilous disguise:
To us a lawn— to hens, a killing ground.

And so it is, my love, with you and me—
This old fool's eyes were ever drawn to youth;
While Nature's Art lies not in what we see,
Such 'seeing' smooths the wilderness of truth.

Though as for that, no truth was ever known
To topple skin-deep Beauty from her throne.

25

WARWICKSHIRE, 2006

Hooked seed or bur of goosegrass, Galium.

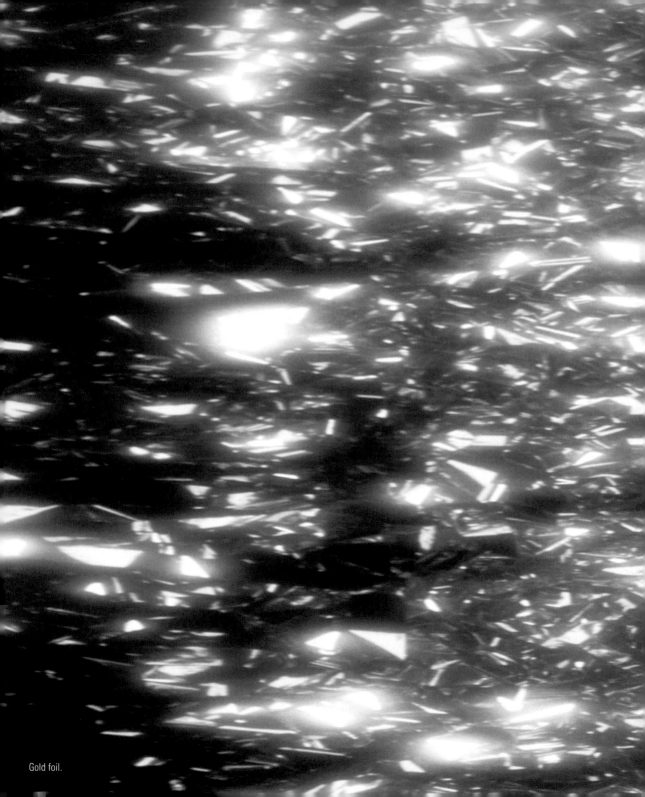

Gold foil.

Do Not Fear the Dark

Fear no goblin mischief,
  Heed no demon bark;
Wrap the night about you tight—
  Do not fear the dark.

Tame the mares of chaos,
  Brand them with your mark;
Leap astride their backs and ride—
  Do not fear the dark.

Float in safety's shadow,
  Sheltering the spark;
Senses bloom within its womb—
  Do not fear the dark.

Long before the founding
  Darkness was the ark,
From its snout the stars spilled out—
  Do not fear the dark.

27

NEW YORK CITY, 2005

Polite Notice

'Include me out'

Include me out— and please excuse
A harmless drudge, who must refuse
To join with those who wish to schmooze,
Or drown their worldly cares in booze,
Or form a choir to sing the blues,
Or watch the television news,
Or dance on tables if they choose.
Consider me a Howard Hughes,
A martyr to my tyrant muse—
Tonight, (in fact, on every night):
Include me out.
And let me write.

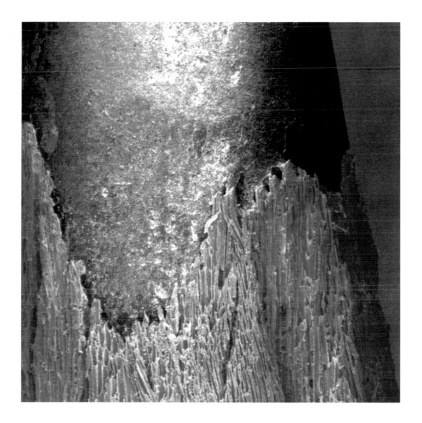

On behalf of writers the world over, I provide the notice opposite which may be copied and affixed in an appropriate spot. It won't work, of course. Nothing is more certain to bring friends or loved ones hammering on your door than the thought that you may be having more fun *on your own in there* (wherever 'there' is) than they are having with the world's distractions at their fingertips.

Tip of a sharpened pencil.

Moon rising over a rocky coastline.

Seven Tides

The first and second tides bleat soft, like sheep;
So soft are they, their waters barely creep
Past infant castles patted in a heap.
The third grows breasts and bristles on the neap;
Upon the fourth our fortunes toss and leap;
The wicked fifth claims what we thought to reap.
The sixth arrives by stealth, while greybeards sleep.
The seventh tide: short terrors — and the deep.

WEST INDIES, 2006

Love is a Loaded Taser

Love is a loaded taser
    Pointed at my heart;
A finger falters... squeezes... fires
A jolt of pain and joy on wires,
To spear me with its razor
    Sharpened dart.
Love knows nothing of our desires,
Nor cares which corpses crowd its shrine:
Whose finger loosed this bolt of
    Love but mine?

40,000 FT OVER GREENLAND, 2005

32

taser: trademark: a weapon firing
barbs attached by wires to batteries,
causing temporary paralysis.
— **New Oxford Dictionary of English**
(Oxford University Press, 1998)

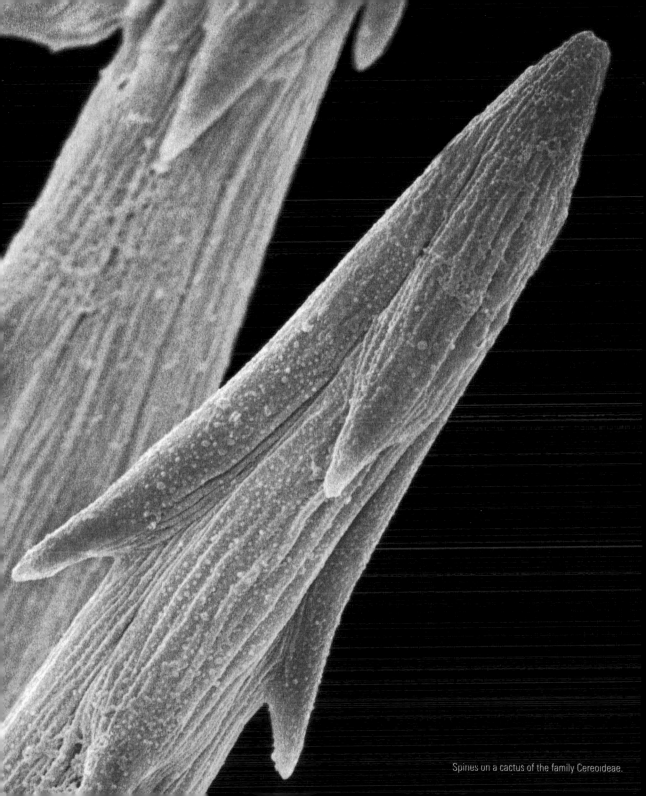

Spines on a cactus of the family Cereoideae.

'World is lunatic...'

World is lunatic, his grass as crazed
As any counterfeit Napoleon
Found raving in his cell— each blade amazed
To hear their cousin reeds' aeolian
Rebellion, whispering in minor key
Across the steppe: *'Join us and learn to sing,*
Mute fodder for the herds— cry mutiny!
Join us!' As mad as any warring king
Who builds himself a cage to call a throne.
World's bones, beneath unquiet seas, thrust up
New monuments of twisted rock and stone,
His mountain lakes a mocking victor's cup
To toast the Sky in sulphur and in flame.
And Sky himself, then not to be outdone,
Brings ruin to those puny cairns of fame
Erected by some long forgotten son
Of long forgotten tribes with storm and wrack,
The patient, endless scrape of wind and sand,
Hard rains and hail to flood such bric-a-brac
Down, down to the sea— and so reclaim the land.

World is lunatic, demented in his bliss;
Even the stars — though pitiless — know this.

WEST INDIES, 2005

Lava flow.

Sand dunes in Death Valley, California.

The Road is Made by Walking

The road is made by walking,
    Abreast or single file.
While idlers sit there gawking, child,
    Come walk with me a while.

No miles are made by talking,
    No map can stride a mile.
The road is made by walking, child,
    Come walk with me a while.

WARWICKSHIRE, 2005

"Wanderer, your footsteps are the road,
  and nothing more;
  wanderer, there is no road, the road
  is made by walking."
    — **Antonio Machado, (1875-1939)**

Volcanic ice cave.

Standing by the Grave

Was there much pain?
Not much.
A little when I could not find the door.

The door to where?
The door...
The door to being loved. A weary climb.

You found love then?
Oh yes.
As much as I deserved— and maybe more.

Behind the door?
No, no.
I had it on my person all the time.

WEST INDIES, 2007

Dorothy's Song

Our *intellects* are mirrored prison stalls,
   Our *common sense* the warden by the door.
Dead men's graffiti, scribbled on the walls,
   Is *reason's* legacy— and nothing more.

The *wisdom of the ancients*— never was,
   For they were men; and men are ruled by *fear*.
The tin man had no heart, there was no OZ,
   And *truths*, like wizards, play each tune by ear.

WARWICKSHIRE, 2005

40

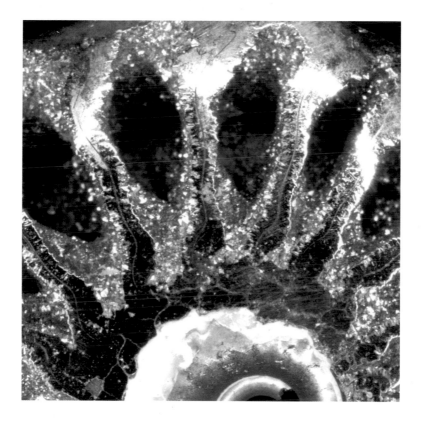

Ammonite fossil.

Poisonous spines of a crown of thorns starfish.

On Hating

There is a place for hating—
Venom spewed out hot,
And then a space for waiting,
When hating is forgot.

There is a time for loathing—
Honest men may rant,
And then a time for clothing
Such honesty in cant.

There is a day for threading
Dunce's caps of shame,
And then a day for shedding
The albatross of blame.

As thorns may not be trusted
To exit from within,
So hate itself— encrusted,
Becomes the greater sin.

WEST INDIES, 2007

'Those evils that inflame the imagination and make
the heart sick, ought not to leave the head cool.'
— **William Hazlitt** 'On the Pleasure of Hating'

'The vet just called...'

January 9, 2008   7:05 P.M.

The vet just called. It's cancer —
Cancer of the bone,
The right-side rear femur —
Here I sit, alone,

Aware I spoke too calmly,
Ashamed I cannot cry.
Two lines of Gerald Manley's
Hymn to Him on high

Sicken my mind. It's cancer —
Cancer of the bone.
No hope. A fist of armour
Wraps my heart in stone.

WEST INDIES, 2008

(For my tiny white lap cat, Molly who died, purring
to the last, six months later in our linen room.)

44

Surface of a cancer cell.

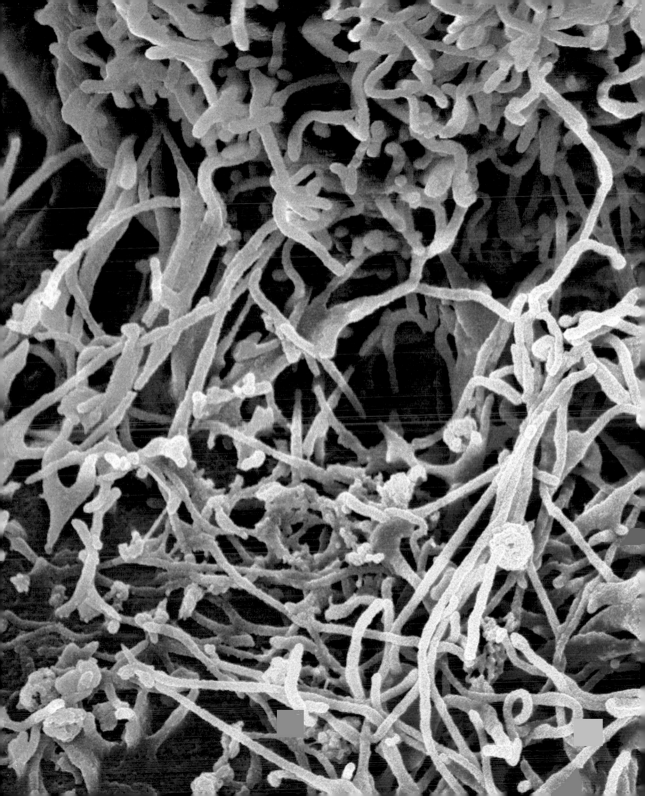

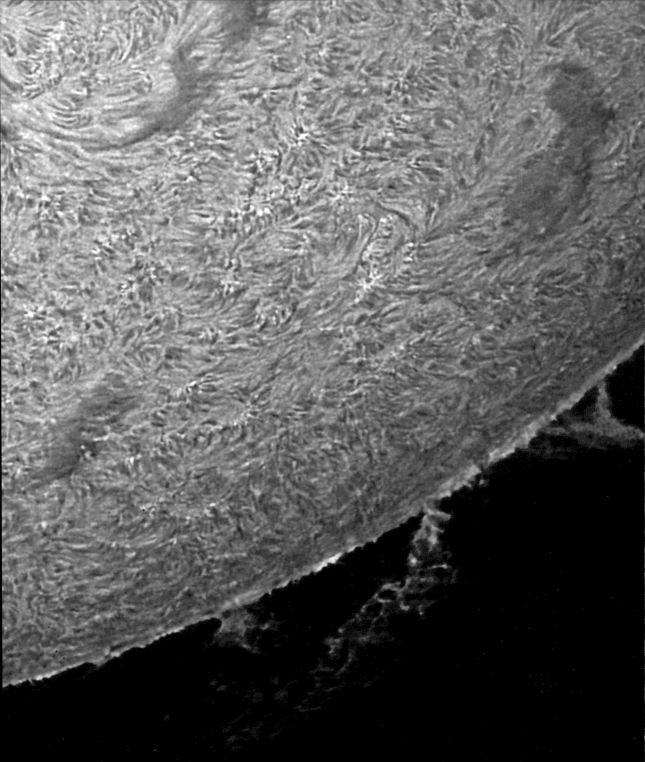

Soaring arcs of gas called prominences leap off the sun with the energy of ten million valcanoes.

April 15, 2007 7:45 p.m.

A glowing, black-boughed cherry
In glory on the lawn,
Stands stripped of leaf or berry,
It's wind-whipped blossom borne

As if in mute defiance
Of what I cannot know —
For neither wit nor science
Could match this matchless show —

As now the sun creeps, laden
With orange, twilight fire,
To kiss this white-lipped maiden —
And, awe-struck, I retire.

WARWICKSHIRE, 2007

Why I Don't Kill Flies

The dog is splayed across the rug,
  Her nose tucked in her paw,
She dreams of hidey-holes long dug,
  Of bones she'll never gnaw.

The cat is curled up in his chair,
  A prisoner of the rain,
His eye meets mine, a slotted stare,
  Contemptuous, half-insane.

A fly squats on my saucer rim
  To rub his leper's legs,
I tense a hand to flatten him
  Or drown him in the dregs,

But cat and dog and fly— we four
  Are hostages to strife,
Each prisoner in our Mother's war—
  The carrier-plague called 'life'...

Which pits each living thing to purge
  Competitors — or die.
I care not what my senses urge:
  I *shall not kill* this fly.

WARWICKSHIRE, 2007

48

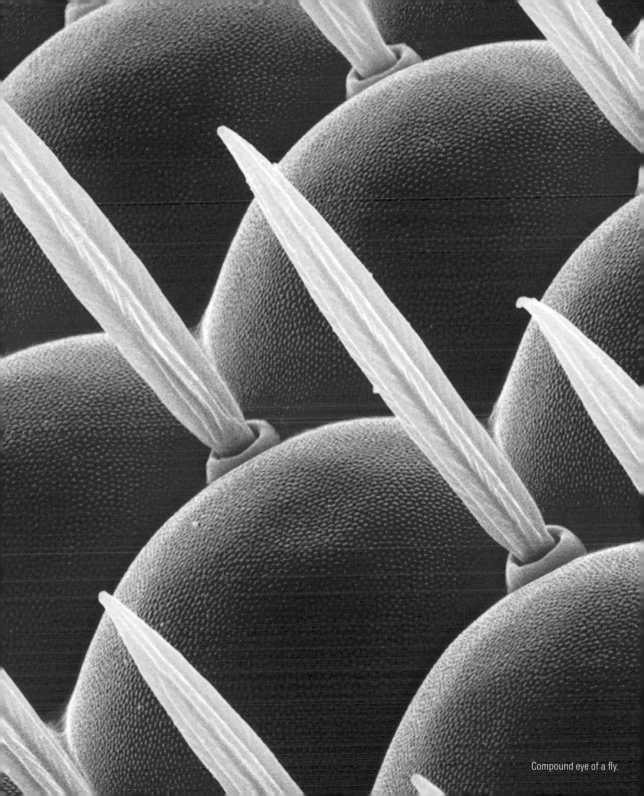

Compound eye of a fly.

Things Certain

To wolves, all dogs are traitors to the tribe,
    To lovers, all advice is wasted breath,
Each conquering hero denigrates the scribe,
    And lives run on an iron rail to death.

WEST INDIES, 2008

Dog hair on an English pointer.

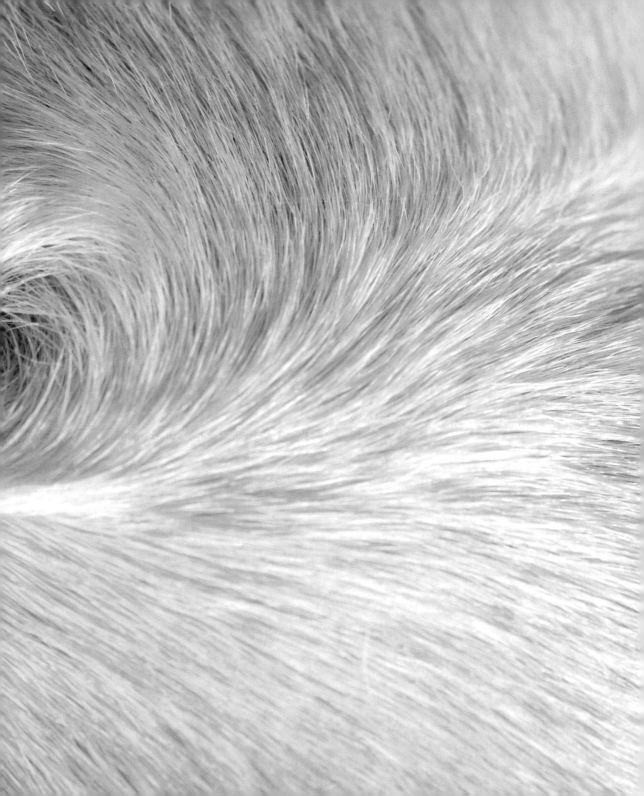

Horsehead Nebula.

The Sleep of Reason

The sleep of reason glories in its shame
And brings forth monsters, hydra-headed fears
We thought long slain; new ghouls to crush and maim
Enlightened truths men once dredged out of tears.
Our age reverts to spell and eye of newt
From fork-tongued wizards, bleating in our ears
Half-lies and righteous cant, which at its root
Hates all it sees, save what its creed reveres.
Sweet dreams! our New Age ayatollahs cry,
The born-again, the thugs, the idiot-proof—
Our reason is that reason now must die!
And so it shall— should we but stand aloof.
    Who cares to sleep while monsters make us slaves,
    With Locke and Newton restless in their graves?

53

WEST INDIES, 2006

A grateful tip of the hat to Francis Wheen and his wonderful book, *How Mumbo-Jumbo Conquered the World: A Short History of Modern Delusions* published in 2004 by Fourth Estate. Buy it, read it and weep. Then join my campaign to have Mr. Wheen made a member of Parliament— against his will, if necessary!

Dear Uncle Felix

Dear Uncle Felix,
I want to be rich like you,
A jet and yacht like the ones *you've* got.
What do I do?

Go and talk to your teacher.
Drown yourself in the moat.
The jet and the yacht I *rent*, you clot.
I enclose a five-pound note.

Dear Uncle Felix,
I want to be rich like you,
The fiver's spent but my bike is bent.
What do I do?

Sell yourself to a pervert.
Write to the police.
Do whatever you think is clever.
Here's twenty quid for some peace.

Dear Uncle Felix,
I want to be rich like you,
My girlfriend's preggers, we live like beggars,
What do I do?

Confess your sins to the vicar.
Subsist on bread and jam.
Batter the cat or eat your hat.
This fifty's for a pram.

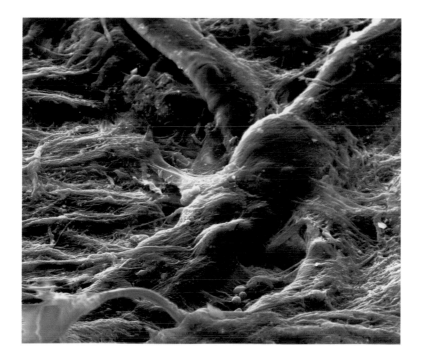

Dear Uncle Felix,
I want to be rich like you,
For a thousand quid you'd be well rid
Of 'What do I do?'

Ah, *blackmail* is it, young 'un?
That's better— let me see.
I admire your cheek, this Monday week
Report to work for me!

WEST INDIES, 2007

With apologies and a respectful tip of a sheepish hat to Allan Ahlberg's
'Please Mrs. Butler' (Kestrel, 1983)

Contaminated banknote.

Forbear, Sir Knight!

Forbear, Sir Knight! You quest too late,
  (Alas, alack for thee);
No damsels in distress now wait
  On shining chivalry.

Your courtly love, your sword and spur
  Bound Guinevere to woe—
And we have learned to much prefer
  The dragon to his foe.

Ride on to lands where maidens cower
  And revel in their plight:
I am the mistress of this tower —
  I am my own heart's knight.

WEST INDIES, 2008

White Desert formations, Egypt.

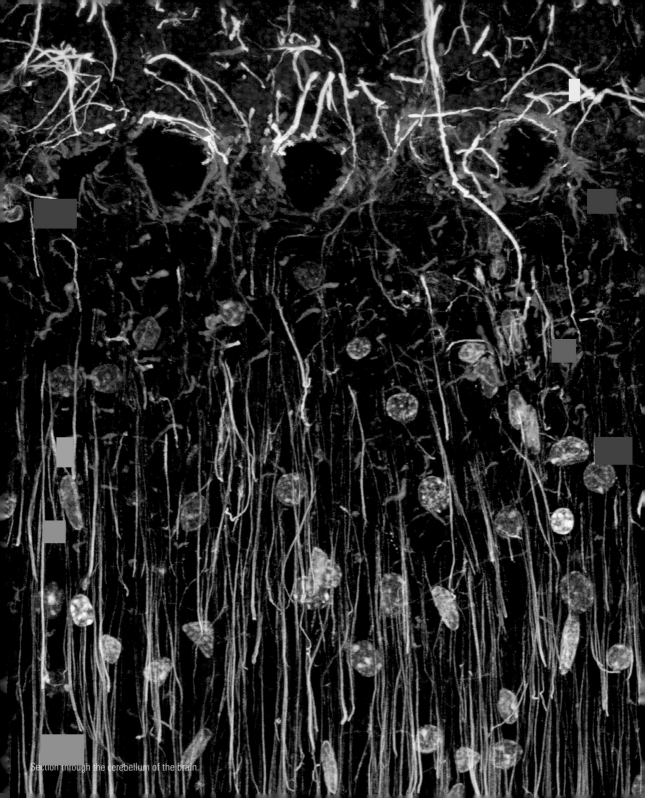

Section through the cerebellum of the brain.

In Search of Ourselves

In search of ourselves— we follow
Wherever the Devil drives,
The hole in our hearts too hollow
To comfort absent lives.

In search of ourselves— we fumble,
Blind in the maze of the mind,
Weighing each blundering stumble,
Fearing what we may find.

In search of ourselves— we scribble,
We pattern and daub and dot,
While the wisest bicker and quibble
To prove what we are not.

In search of ourselves— we wander,
And the bravest stray too far,
And the lost mint coin to squander
To pay for who we are.

In search of ourselves— we murder
And clamour to mourn the dead,
While innocence squats in purdah,
Her hands held to her head.

In search of ourselves— we borrow
The shadow of debts unpaid,
The quest of a needless sorrow
For what has long decayed.

59

'Of *course* you do...'

Roses are red,
Violets are blue,
I hate my parents. *

Of *course* you do— we made this world
Into which you dolts were hurled;
A world where fish swim in the sea
Luminous with mercury—
Where acid rain burns forests out,
Global warming causes drought,
Where perverts lurk beneath your bed,
Kidnap you, and then you're dead—
A world where you think robot thoughts,
Whisked to school in juggernauts,
Dressed to the nines like rap god clones,
Mumbling into mobile phones—
A sluttish world of label snobs,
Food fads, Botox and McJobs,
Where unprotected sex is death,
(Ditto fat or crystal meth),
Where wicked men, (whom you abuse),
Murder cows to make you shoes,
Where children in some far off land
Packed the iPod in your hand
And sweated labour, on the rack,
Faked the T-shirt on your back.
Oh thou! the wretched of the earth
(Who curse the fools who gave you birth),
My generation made all this—
Here's your allowance...
                        give us a kiss.

* Lines by Euan Ferguson in *The Observer*. Or so we are told by the author and harpsichordist, Michael Bywater, in his riveting book *Lost Worlds: What Have We Lost, & Where Did it Go?* (Granta 2004). I used to employ Mr. Bywater as a columnist. He is the sort of writer and thinker who makes you proud to be a publisher. He reminds me of Stephen Fry at the top of his game— and in a very bad mood. Marvellous stuff.

Mercury under harmonic vibration.

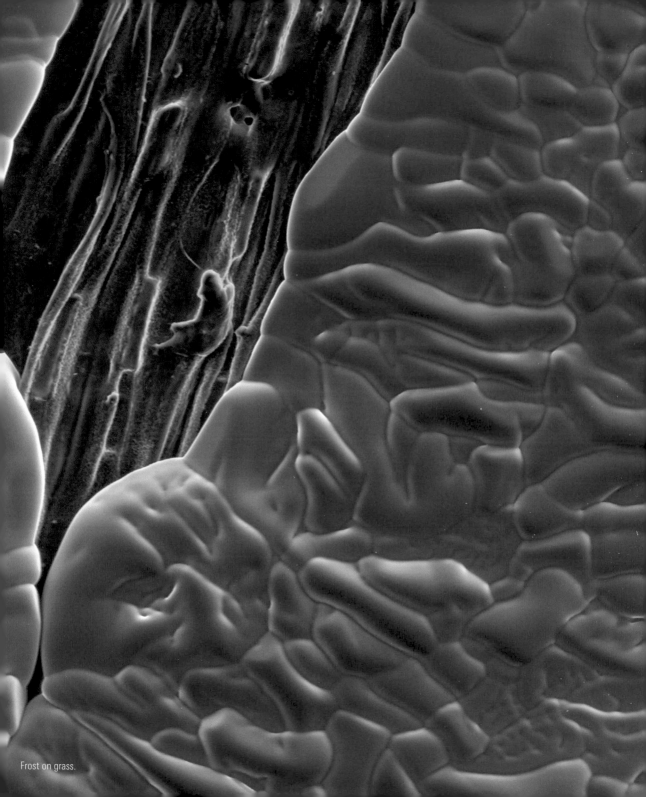
Frost on grass.

Going Bald

My ornamental maples are tenacious;
While oak and alder mourn for what is lost
They sulk in glory, obdurate, ungracious,
Their kamikaze boughs defying frost.

The memory of summer serenades us,
While autumn's fingers tug till we are shorn,
And winter finds us out, and death persuades us
To drop our golden hoard upon the lawn.

WARWICKSHIRE, 2005

63

Komodo dragon skin.

'We are different when we are alone...'

We are different when we are alone,
  When artifice has no use,
When the mask of our laughter is bone
  And the werewolf of self is loose;

As fingernails harden to claws
  And skin to reptilian scale,
As we lope to our bed on all fours,
  And the mirror reveals a tail...

With the birds of community flown,
  We to ourselves grow strange,
We are different when we are alone—
  Like a garden at night, we change.

WARWICKSHIRE, 2005

65

Rude Awakening

I thought I'd die when he asked me out,
I wanted to cry, I wanted to shout,
I wanted my friends to know— to share it,
(And all the rest could grin and bear it),
I wanted those cows who paint their zits
And pout and pose and flaunt their tits
To know that none of them stood a chance,
That he and I were going to dance,
That I'd be wearing no underwear
And I'd tell him, too— so let them stare,
I couldn't care less what anyone said,
And I hoped they'd guess we'd been to bed.

Oh, I thought I'd love him for evermore:
But that was before I *heard him snore!*

WEST INDIES, 2006

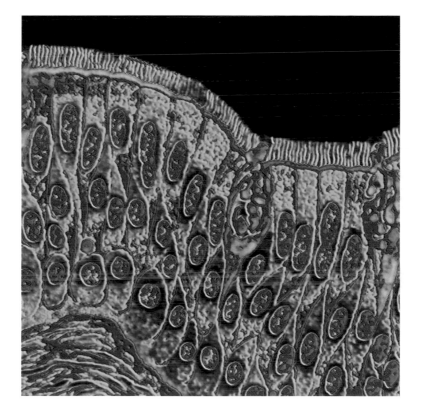

Section through the wall of the human trachea (windpipe) showing ciliated epithelium.

Subatomic particle tracks.

All Will Be Well

As our generation passes
  From summer into fall,
As our tragedies— and farces—
  Lose their power to appal;

As the glory of our raving
  Is dimmed behind a door,
As what we thought worth saving
  Becomes a bloody bore;

As the few became a crowd,
  And the irony a mask,
As the joke is told too loud
  By those who have to ask;

As our dramas shrink to farces
  And our vanities decay,
So our generation passes
  From riot to cliché.

WARWICKSHIRE, 2006

Someone is Missing

(for Patsy Fisher 1932 - 2006)

Someone is missing— a crafter of quiet,
A beacon of love in the midst of riot;

Someone whose laughter scattered the thunder,
Someone who saw through eyes of wonder;

Someone who reckoned hate a blindness,
Someone who smothered fault with kindness;

Someone who wore her learning lightly,
Someone whose gentleness chided us slightly;

Someone who fashioned her heart a palace,
Someone whose innocence walled out malice;

Someone who harnessed hurt to healing,
Someone who knew just how you were feeling;

Someone whose painterly eye saw through you,
Someone who loved you before she knew you;

Someone who never called in her marker:
Someone is missing. And life is darker.

WEST INDIES, 2006

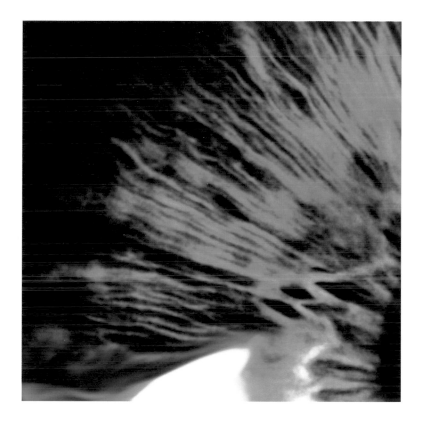

Iris and pupil of an eye.

Confeffion

In poesy, I flaunt fatal flaws,
Preferring 'thou', (or 'thine' to 'yours'),
And though I never stretched to 'thee'
I could have done, believe thou me.
It's just pretentiousneff, one guesses,
Substituting 'ff's for 'ss'es,
Yet, I mourn (like Miniver C)
The rhyming scans that died with 'thee',
And mourn still more the loss of 'thou'
(So helpful when one's bombing Slough);
But as for that, I've sworn an oath
To editors and readers, both,
To clothe my thoughts in modern dreff
And come to love a double 'ss'.

WARWICKSHIRE, 2007

'Miniver cursed the commonplace
And eyed a khaki suit with loathing;
He missed the mediæval grace
Of iron clothing.'

from 'Miniver Cheevy'
— **Edward Arlington Robinson**

'Come friendly bombs and fall on Slough!
It isn't fit for humans now,
There isn't grass to graze a cow.
Swarm over, Death!'

from 'Slough'
— **John Betjeman**

I have noted it publicly before and wish to say again: there is not a *'thee'*, *'thine'* or *'thou'* in my published poetry that my sensible editor, Simon Rae, has not attempted to excise. How right he is, of course, and how grateful I am to him for having broken me (almost) of the habit. And yet...

Bark of the Grecian Strawberry tree.

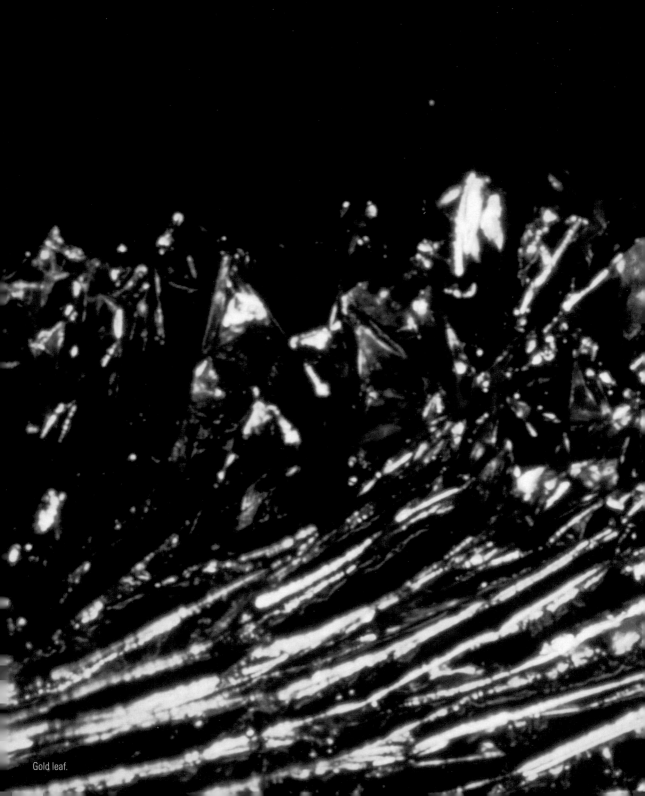

Gold leaf.

'The gods have shown me favour...'

The gods have shown me favour,
  (If any gods there be),
Yet were my nature braver
  I might dispute the fee.

For gold and gold's devices
  Are cloaks before men's eyes,
Their virtues and their vices,
  Breed envy in disguise.

And envy fosters fawning,
  That parasite of trust,
A worm of loathing, spawning
  A plague of self-disgust.

When slaves of acclamation
  Are met, by chance or plan,
We meet a reputation,
  But seldom meet the man—

Fame's amour shines too brightly,
  As once it did for me,
Yet those who wear it lightly,
  In time, may rue the fee.

WARWICKSHIRE, 2005

Conversation with a Child
by 'The Cotton House' Pond

Why do they call them dragonflies?
The only answer is: we do—
The names of things are often lies.
But why do they call them dragonflies?
And are those diamonds in their eyes?
Why, bless you, child, I wish I knew.
So why do they call them dragonflies?
The only answer is: we do.

WEST INDIES, 2006

Triolets are not exactly a popular verse form today— if, indeed, they ever were in English poetry. W. H. Auden apparently thought them too trivial to bother with, and I would bow unhesitatingly to his genius in such matters. But a triolet just sort of happened in the above lines— perhaps it suited the repetitive nature of my young friend's questioning. And anyway, why *are* they called dragonflies?

Compound eyes of dragonfly.

Caged Fire

I always had my way, as you had yours;
Each to the other courteous but firm,
Interpreters of verdicts, codes and laws,
Of jurisdiction, penalty and term,
Softening confrontation where we could—
Our love no less for that and no less rash
Than vulgar fires of paraffin and wood
That blaze a while and then subside to ash.
A widened eye served notice of dissent;
A slight embrace, apology in full;
A short 'Good night' to signal discontent;
Our bed the only site of push and pull.
   The world misunderstood such lack of show:
   Serenity without— caged fire below.

WEST INDIES, 2006

Rosette Nebula emission.

Bone surface, showing lacuna (holes).

'For those who know it isn't true...'

For those who know it isn't true,
No matter if we wanted to,
Who kick and fume against the pricks
Of bearded rogues and dirty tricks,
Of costumed ranters casting stones
While venerating piles of bones
And fetching wood to burn old crones...

For those who stood against the fear,
Or those that ran, but held the rear,
Who fought a creeping worm of shame,
Who sought no other fool to blame,
Who read the book and thought it through
And wanted to believe, but knew,
Most likely, that it wasn't true...

For those who snuffed the candle out
To wander, lost, in caves of doubt,
Who face what we each know must come,
Who fear, and yet will not succumb
To blandishments or threats, who cry:
'You preach that heretics must die,
If what you say is true— then *why?*'

Men's gods were born of Man's own dread,
A dread that seeks its own twin dead,
And as faith waned— your hatred grew
For those who know it isn't true.

WEST INDIES, 2007

My Advice

(For my God-daughter— or anybody's daughter)

You're deep in love, his love is true,
He's never met a girl like you,
And though I hope he never will,
My own advice is— *take the pill.*

And when you wed, you silly thing,
Demand a big fat diamond ring,
For when you're old and fat and lame
A diamond loves you— *just the same.*

Though you might rather die if he
Died tragically at twenty-three,
Take my advice and while you're calm
Get life insurance— *where's the harm?*

Though hand in hand and side by side
You turn to face life's rising tide,
And he loves you and you love him:
Take my advice— *and learn to swim.*

WARWICKSHIRE, 2006

The etched surface of a microdiamond crystal from Siberia, Russia.

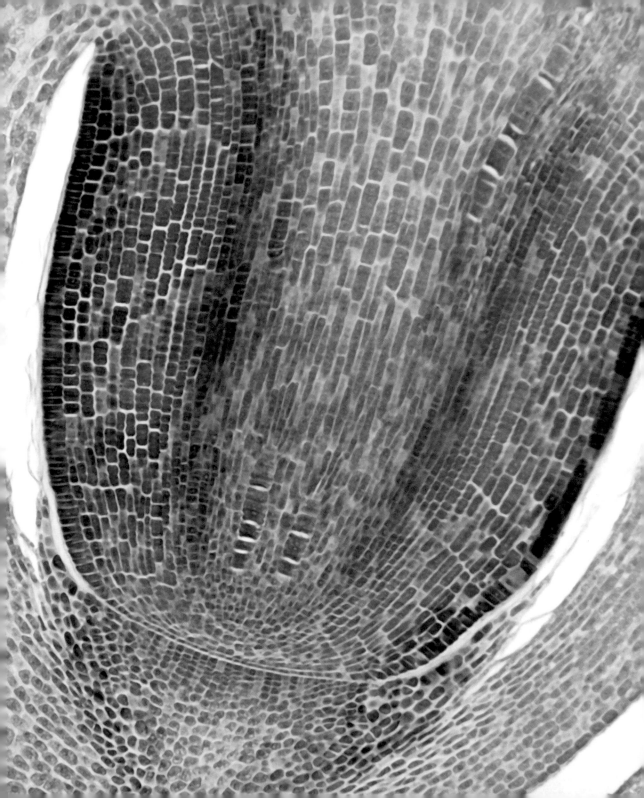

Perfect Day

Today was one of the best days of my life.
Nothing of any importance occurred—
I cut my finger on a paperknife
And marvelled at a busy hummingbird
Plucking out wet moss by a waterfall;
Broke bread with friends and shared a glass of wine;
Wrote this poem; swam; made love. That's all.
Why should it be some days erect a shrine,
A cairn, a white stone day, in memory?
Is it, as Buddhists claim, a lack of need,
Or want— or simple serendipity —
The perfect flowering of one small seed?
   The wise will say our frames are none too pure:
   How many perfect days could we endure?

WEST INDIES, 2007

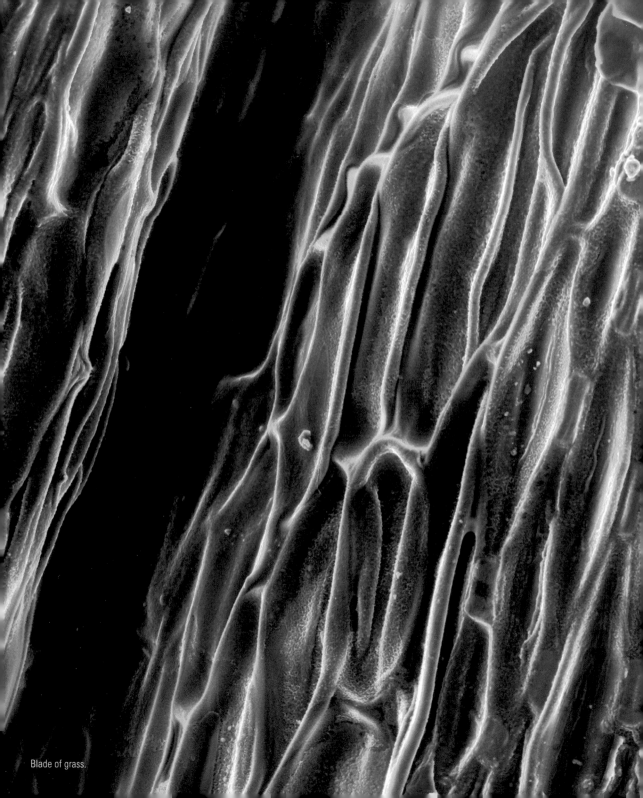
Blade of grass.

'I watched you while you slept...'

I watched you while you slept—
Careless of flesh and bone,
Difficult to accept,
A year or so and you'll be grown
Too old for me to chide,
Too wise for me to warn—
From today the downhill slide
Begins— a startled fawn
Will seek a grass much greener
Upon another hill,
Lands where the air is keener,
Where magic lingers still.
But do not take the nearest—
Dear God, my heart would burst:
With all your getting, dearest,
Get understanding first.

WEST INDIES, 2006

Kamchatka coast.

Song for a Child, Newly Born

May your thoughts be with the living,
  May your hand and eye be swift,
May your thanks be with the giving
  And never with the gift.

May your kindness be unfailing,
  May your ship glide by each shoal,
May the helmsman of each sailing
  Be the captain of your soul.

May you pass through all life's dangers,
  May your lovers all be true,
May you learn that this world's strangers
  Were friends you never knew.

May your laughter ring like fountains,
  May your heart be wild and free,
May you walk among the mountains
  But live beside the sea.

WEST INDIES, 2004

'THE NOVELIST'

Our Writers' Group was having fits,
    A NOV-EL-IST was coming
To lecture us — to stir our wits —
    It set our juices humming!

The great man staggered in, half-pissed,
    By Joyce! it was exciting:
"You wish to be A NO-VEL-IST —
    Why, then, are you not *writing*?"

WEST INDIES, 2007

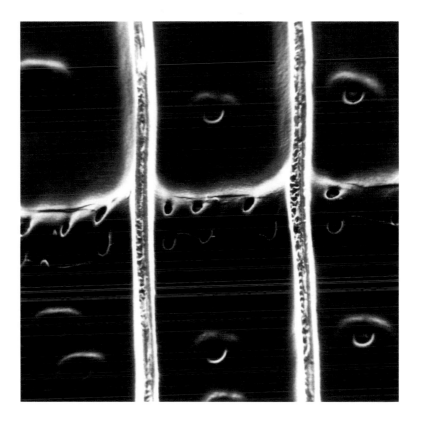

Xylem, the supporting and water-conducting tissue of vascular plants, of a redwood.

Fossilised scales of the bony fish, Dapedium sp.

A Saturday Gig

(off the M1, 1964)

Crammed in a van like tinned sardines,
Three in the front and three in the rear,
Our stage shirts on the roadie's lap,
Fingers tracing the route on the map
With Pete's harmonica in our ear:
The night is young in Milton Keynes!

Then after the gig, still hyped, half dead,
Half deaf, we help the roadie load,
And flirt with girls: 'We think yer great!'
(Perhaps we were.) 'Let's go. It's late!'
'Drop me off at the top of the road.'
'G'night.''G'night.' And an empty bed.

WEST INDIES, 2006

'But'

What continents that muttered word can span,
  The '*u*' an aqueduct for *b*liss or *t*ears,
A bridge of knives between 'cannot' and 'can',
  A cantilevered hope with rotten piers.

WEST INDIES, 2007

95

Salt lakes, channels and deposits in the Carrizo Plain National Monument, California, USA.

Voyager 2 image of Jupiter, showing Great Red Spot.

Death of an Author

Come in! I thought it might be you,
Hoping it would not be true,
Though hope has little purchase here—
And has not had this many a year:
There's FATE, your old familiar owl,
(I see her, peeking through your cowl),
FREE WILLIE'S fangs locked on your coat—
The Lie of Lies lodged in his throat.
Come in, come in! Bring out your list,
Set down that blade and rest your wrist,
I fear we have no time to dine
But let me finish up this wine—
The last, I think, that I shall drink?
(My word, does foul FATE never blink?)

➤

There now! And I assume you bring
What James called 'the distinguished thing',
Though Henry's creed on what was what
Was 'judge all potters by their pot'
And damn the mess — his dainty knife
Could never hack the clay of life...
Excuse this rambling — terror maims
The intellect, as false hope shames
An athlete passed his punch-drunk prime...
Yes quite. You have so little time.
FREE WILL is slithering down your seam
And I (transfixed within this dream)
Must watch her bite a nerveless vein
On legs that shall not lift again.
So be it. Has she finished yet?
FREE WILL, indeed— a loathsome pet
Whose mother slept in Eden's tree
And served young Eve as he serves me,
As you, in turn, on rattling limbs
Still serve your deathless master's whims.

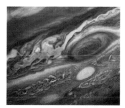

'Tis done? Then I shall rack my brains
For words: 'a drowsy numbness pains...'
No, no; I'll spout no stolen sweets,
(I never cared too well for Keats,
His song so rich it lacked the fire
To plumb the depths of real desire);
How's this: 'Though all must come to grief
And loss, I seek no false relief
In superstition's stinking rod —
I'll take my chance — you keep your God
Or gods — though I admired your book —
I'll hang my hat on Housman's hook,
A second-rater though he be,
My last thoughts are: his cherry tree,
Emily's coach and Browning's bride—
With Will's dark lady by her side!

WEST INDIES, 2008

Homo sapiens sapiens
(Wisest of the wise)

Today, in a picture book, I saw
A frog with a bat gripped in its maw,
Two tiny legs hung out to dry,
Beneath a gold reptilian eye—

An eye that spoke of empty Zen
Spawned long before the dawn of men,
An eye that will be staring still
When London sleeps beneath a hill.

But of the bat, the lens was mute,
Death falls silent in pursuit,
And we may learn — to our surprise —
Just who was 'wisest of the wise'.

WEST INDIES, 2007

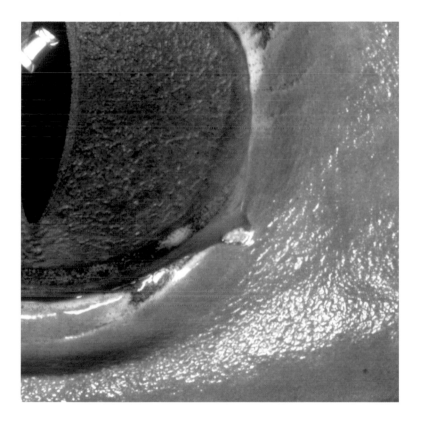

The eye of a tree frog.

Patterns in cooled pahoehoe lava, Kilauea, Hawaii.

Of Doubts

Of doubts, the world can boast its sure despisers,
   The men of right or wrong, of black or white,
Who hoard up stones, implacable as misers,
   To cast at shade of grey and slake their spite.

So sure are they that pelting small transgressors
   Will furnish them a shield: 'You stinking whore!'
'You idle brute!'— they set up as confessors,
   Each warranted to preach God's truth, God's law.

When one such entered heaven, he derided
   The slum the angels proffered: 'Ah,' they shrilled,
'But this was the material provided —
   Your sent us so few bricks with which to build.'

   When fools are certain — there all justice ends:
   Store up your doubts and treasure them as friends.

WEST INDIES, 2007

103

Interlude

I don't know you— you don't know me,
This happenstance is all we know,
Yet rivers still embrace a sea
Whose creatures sing strange songs below.

You don't know me— what could you know?
And have your dragons all been slain?
Say nothing! — while our hearts pound so
To drown within each others' pain.

WEST INDIES, 2007

Zooplankton colony. Pacific Ocean, southern California.

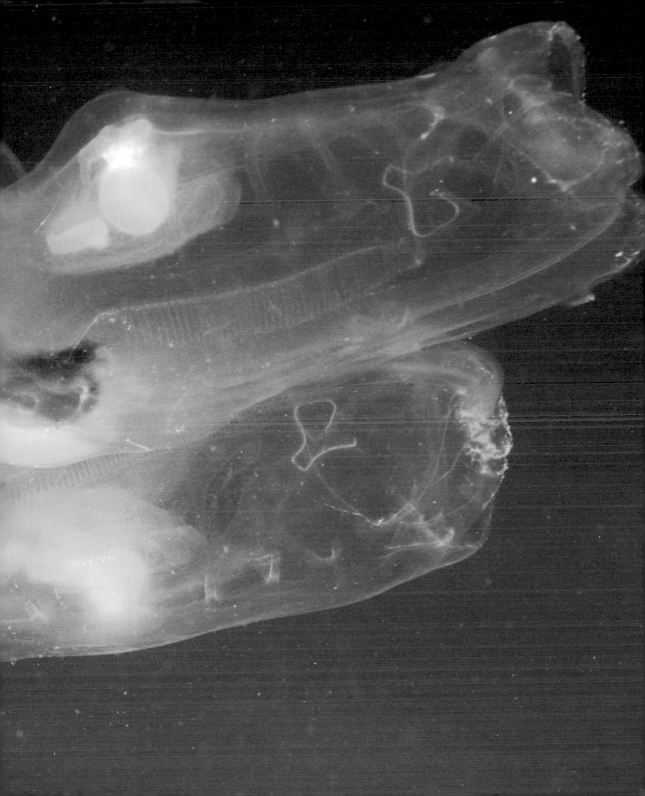

Cave of Crystals, Naica Mine, Mexico.

'I mined in seams of pleasure...'

I mined in seams of pleasure
To pick apart its ore,
I found no shards of treasure,
Of pleasure, little more.

Ah, there are they who tell me
I lacked a map or chart,
(And they have one to sell me!)
Yet I have not the heart

To tell them: '...as you wander
In tunnels for your pay,
Be careful— lest you squander
Your hope and youth away.'

WEST INDIES, 2007

When Parent Speaks to Child

The past is ever present when parent speaks to child,
    The double-entry errors of elders reconciled;
In vain you swear *your* children will suffer no such crime:
    Your mother rocks the baby, content to bide her time.

WARWICKSHIRE, 2007

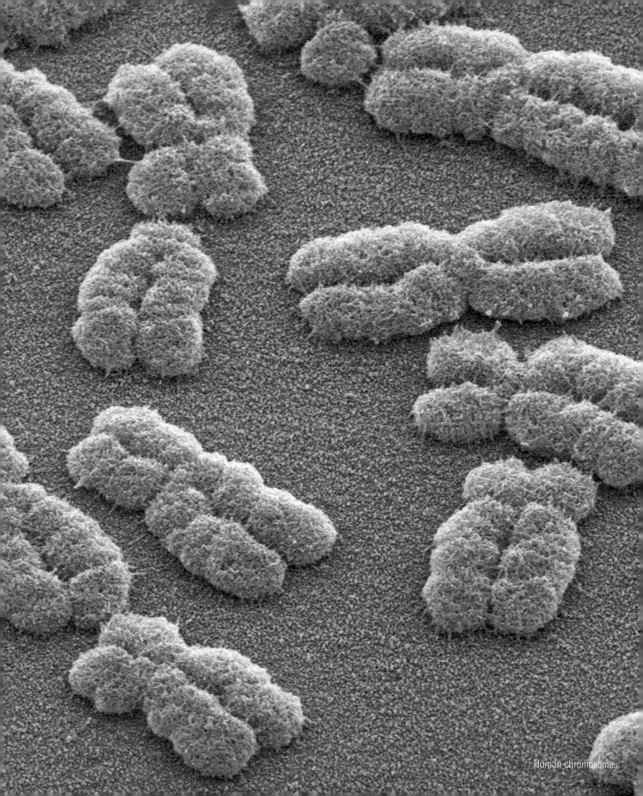

Human chromosomes.

A Love Forbidden

Through doors we never opened,
　Where time hung on a thread,
On beds the gods had tested
　When they were newly wed;

Within a place of silence,
　Dark angels overhead,
We signed the Book of Martyrs
　Which He alone has read;

In rooms we never entered,
　Where wisdom feared to tread,
We pledged our love, undying,
　With words we never said.

43,000 FT OVER THE ATLANTIC, 2006

Desert oases, United Arab Emirates.

Moss spore capsule.

Poets Anonymous

"My name is Felix and I am a poet.
I became a poet five years ago
Following an illness. Of course, that's no
Excuse—the illness, I mean. I know.

We know about the world poets inhabit—
The wreckage their behaviour brings to wives,
Husbands, children, etc. How the habit
Sours and decimates our loved-ones' lives,

Eating up time we could be spending
Late at the office, earning a crust
To pay for our children's mobile phone bills.
Or watching TV with the family. We must

Be honest with ourselves. Think of the horrible
Embarrassment of a loved one forced to say:
'Well, to be honest, he/she is a poet.'
The appalled silence as they turn away.

We know all that. How we break promises
To take up stamp collecting. We know it,
Locked away in our own little selfish world.
My name is Felix and I am a poet."

WEST INDIES, 2005

113

'We have no rights...'

We have no rights— except those born in tears;
And blood; and sweat; the bitter fruit of battle,
The gnawing at the heart of martyr's fears
Whose names we do not even know. The rattle
In their welling throats; the heel taps of the wracked;
Their screams as lumps of living flesh were tortured,
Burnt and scalded, dislocated, pierced and hacked
By Men of God— their masters in the orchard...
'My dear Archbishop, try another pear,
The cherry trees are sweeter by the chapel,
These heretics will soon repent, I swear.
Or would your Grace perhaps prefer an apple?'
  We Have No Rights! but what we took by threat:
  They long to snatch them back, should we forget.

WEST INDIES, 2004

Scalding mud pots, Sol de Manana

Saturns rings showing spokes.

Dementia

Lord, spare me from the emptiness of days,
From knowledge half remembered, half concealed;
From knowing winks that greet me in the maze,
From what lies in the pit — unshrived, unhealed.

Lord save me from the stench of bowel and tract,
From nurses with their hearty cries and broth,
From surgeons with their jargon and their tact,
Lord send me strength to vent a mighty wrath

Annihilating pity and its kind,
From condescending fools who crowd my bed —
Lord grant me one clear day with clearer mind
In which to make my peace. Then strike me dead.

A day of laughter, friendship, joy and wit;
Just one clear day — and then fulfill Thy writ.

WEST INDIES, 2006

Scales from the skin of a shark.

'I place more trust in kindliness...'

I place more trust in kindliness
   Than honesty or pride,
Though as for that, all trust, I guess,
   Is not so deep or wide

As we should like to think: it's thread
   Once rent, is snatched away,
Yet kindliness, with love half-dead,
   Still makes a tourniquet.

While as for pride, an armoured suit
   Is more its metaphor,
It has its uses in dispute
   With blackguards at the door.

Curt honesty, loosed from its sheath,
   Will cut both friend and foe,
Its coat of arms, a quartered wreath
   Upon a field of woe.

Each virtue's armament and art
   Turns traitor, overdone;
Commit to kindliness — dear heart —
   If you must choose just one.

WEST INDIES, 2006

Misspent

I had no youth worth speaking of
With both hands in the fire;
My eyes were fixed on prizes then,
The idols of desire:

My Apple suit, two kilim rugs,
Chrome furniture from Heals,
A Biba shawl tossed on the couch,
A nodding pope on wheels;

The painted tie from Mr. Fish,
A meditation mat,
White bootlegs from the USA,
Pete Townshend's shattered Strat';

The Hockney print that cost too much,
The fancy deck by Linn,
A wooden box carved in Nepal
To keep the Smarties in;

Star formation.

Young goddess sluts to carry home
From Middle Earth or Tramp,
Sharp's Dylan poster in the loo
Disguising rising damp;

Some copper's helmet in the hall
To prove my streetwise cred,
Soft shadows from a lava lamp
Across the waterbed;

My leather jacket, 'Angel patched'—
God, I was such a liar:
I had no youth worth speaking of...
With both hands in the fire.

WEST INDIES, 2005

'Apple', 'Biba', 'Mr. Fish', 'white bootlegs', 'Strat', 'Linn,
'Sharp'... all meaningless, I'm afraid, unless you happened
to be living in London in the late 1960's or early 1970's.
But they meant something to us; they meant you were
cool. In Bobby Dylan's immortal phrase, they meant
'something is happening here, but you don't know what
it is — do you, Mr. Jones?'

Eight Deadly Sins

Pride, a wreck where hope once stood—
Envy, grief for a neighbour's good—
Cant and anger bring to **Wrath**
Defective love, the root of **Sloth**—

Weak-kneed **Avarice** covets all—
While **Gluttony** grooms **Lust** to crawl
Beside him, trembling, bathed in sweat—
Lord cleanse thy servant, but not yet!

WEST INDIES, 2006

Sea slug, Halgerda batangas.

These are the seven deadly (or capital) sins as distinguished by Pope Gregory in the 6th century, in order of severity, starting with **Pride**, 'the beginning of every sin'. To Gregory's seven I have added an eighth: Augustine's sin of **Prevarication** summed up in book 8 of his *Confessions* three centuries earlier: '[Lord,] give me chastity and continence, but not yet'. Which, I guess, is how most of us feel on that subject most of the time. As to 'Defective love, the root of sloth', this came from my reading of a translation of Aquinas in which he argues that all sins are derived, one way and another, from love, and that 'sloth is grief for Divine, spiritual love.' This sounds like baloney, until you read his powerful argument.

Sweeper fish shoal.

More

More them in the world than we.
More lock in the world than key.

More sky in the world than roof.
More why in the world than proof.

More dirt in the world than soap.
More hurt in the world than hope.

More need in the world than how.
More weed in the world than plough.

More walk in the world than shoe.
More talk in the world than do.

More bark in the world than bite.
More dark in the world than light.

More shame in the world than pride.
More lame in the world than ride.

More stick in the world than eat.
More trick in the world than treat.

More fake in the world than friend.
More break in the world than mend.

More fish in the world than net.
More wish in the world than get.

More lock in the world than key.
More them in the world than we.

WEST INDIES, 2006

Any Farmer to Any Bishop

As cause begets effect— so men make wine
(A new excuse to bathe in its applause),
Young puppies roar that virgins' eyes may shine—
And each effect, in turn, begets new cause.

Yet were this flock to seek your canting calm,
You preachly fool, who then would thresh the corn?
Your tithe came from the labour of my arm,
These fields were here before your church was born.

For fear of forfeit, Pascal's Wagers stand,
But who are you to bleat of sheep and goat
Whose gaudy crook would shame a shepherd's hand,
Whose consolations tumble out by rote?

   As cause begets effect and men make riot,
   So parasites should suck their blood— in quiet!

WARWICKSHIRE, 2007

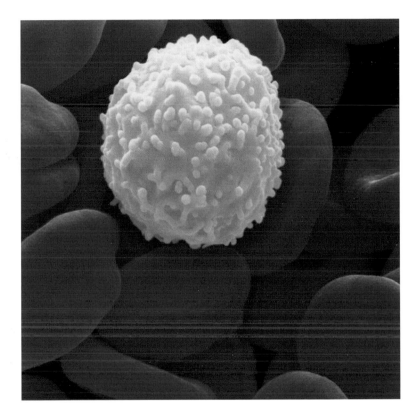

'Pascal's Wagers' French philosopher, mathematician, probability theorist and scientist Blaise Pascal (1623-1662) argued that as we do not (and cannot) know whether God exists, then we should play it safe rather than risk the consequences of denying God's existence. Thus 'Pascal's Wagers' are an attempt to justify belief in God not with an appeal to evidence for God's existence but rather with an appeal to self-interest. Despite having been refuted many times, his arguments remain a potent inducement to believe for the fearful and the credulous.

Human red and white blood cells.

Apollo 17 orbital image of the large crater Sarabhai, on the Moon.

'Where is my enemy..?'

[M.T. 1946 - 2005]

Where is my enemy, the beast I sought
To quarter limb from limb; to choke and rend?
I batter at infinities of nought,
For though I scour the world from end to end,
Entreating: 'Death where are you? Death come out!'
He will not come. No news, no answer, save
An echo from the hills, a knife-thin shout
To lance the heart of mourners by your grave.
Where is my enemy, the old, old foe?
I asked the sea, the mountains and the moon,
The birds and beasts, the earth— they do not know;
Except, they say, we each shall find him soon:
    'He has no need of hidden lairs or hells,
    Within each living thing, in part, he dwells.'

WARWICKSHIRE, 2005

Creation Myth

And Man so sinned, a creeping guilt
  Invaded his domain,
And Man said: *Let machines be built*
  With which to mask our pain;

Machines to sing in roaring choirs,
  To lull the world with noise,
Sweet orphans of our own desires—
  The tyrants of our joys.

WEST INDIES, 2008

Optical fibres.

Upon the Beach

Upon the beach a solitary tree
   Defies the sea— a shambling stag at bay,
The left side iridescent greenery,
   The right a driftwood copse of salt and spray.

I wade from where the living sap still thrives
   To stroke an antlered bough worn white as bone:
Wet sand sucks at my feet— so time sucks lives,
   The concubine reduced to chaperone.

What lightning strike was this, what storm or wrack
   Wrought ruin with a hydra-headed glance?
Half-naked, with the crab grass at her back,
   She stands, as we must stand, a shrine to chance.

   So ravaged kings on crutches play their part,
   And ghosts of faded beauty stir the heart.

WEST INDIES, 2008

Rippled sand dunes, United Arab Emirates.

The Walls of Time

Pried from the fortress walls of time
Unsought, a fragment falls,
Freed from a shard of mortared mime
A lost friend's laughter calls.

Here are the days of fearsome youth
Entombed in stone and silt,
Proud towers of what passed for truth
Marooned in moats of guilt.

Rewritten mounds of wrecked debris
Hold looted, broken spoil,
While tilled fields men called memory
Revert to virgin soil.

WEST INDIES, 2007

134

Cut and polished agate surface.

An Older England

There has always been in England
  An older England still,
Where Chaucer rode to Canterbury
  And Falstaff drank his fill.

Where poets scrawled immortal lines
  Beside a daffodil,
And lovers lay upon the grass
  Atop of Bredon Hill.

Where parson in his pulpit droned
  As Nancy winked at Bill,
Where Brontës conjured moonlit paths
  And Hardy drowned a mill.

Where jolly tars sailed hearts-of-oak
  From China to Brazil,
And foxes sought out Squire's pack
  To race them for the thrill.

We never could cease worshipping
  What never was— nor will;
There has always been in England
  An older England still.

WEST INDIES, 2005

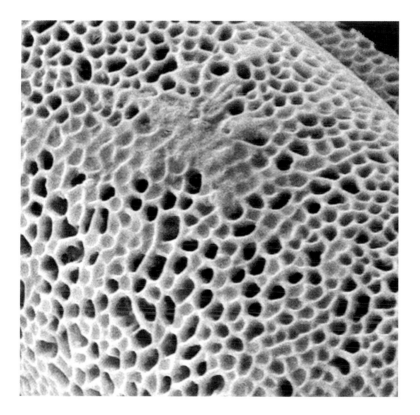

"I think Shakespeare was greatly preoccupied... with the loss of innocence and I think there has always been in England an older England, which was sweeter and purer, where the hay smelled better and the weather was always springlike and the daffodils blew in gentle warm breezes."

— **Orson Welles**, near the end of his life, talking about Falstaff to the BBC

Daffodil pollen grain.

Mudflats in the North Sea, off the coast of Pellworm Island, Germany.

Two of a Kind

Against the greenhouse glass, out in the yard,
An ardent partridge stabs his own reflection,
While I sit scribbling — hammering just as hard
At non-existent wraiths of self-deception.

WARWICKSHIRE, 2008

Liposome vesicles.

Habit

Dearest, we grew careless by degrees,
Drugged with love's familiarities,
Better it were malice
Poisoning the chalice
Habit bid us swallow to the lees.

Custom courts enslavement in disguise,
Usage hastens love to its demise,
Fading to a glimmer
As the light grew dimmer—
Habit wound a blindfold round our eyes.

WARWICKSHIRE, 2006

'When all strings sever...'

When all strings sever, leaving one thin thread
And infant tyrannies of need reverse,
Then love must bite its tongue and turn its head.

Where once it strode abroad, it now must tread
As softly as a carpet-slippered nurse.
When all strings sever, leaving one thin thread,

When seas of darkness cover what is fled
And you must swim beside an empty hearse,
Your love must smile and sweetly turn its head.

Nor may you hail the ship, its slack sails spread
Upon a course to bloody grief or worse
With all lines severed, save for one thin thread.

As Ahab rants that Ishmael is dead
Make no reply, for love is in the curse
And love may smile, but may not turn its head.

Hold fast the line— forgetting what was said,
Our lives are not a voyage that we rehearse.
When all strings sever, leaving one thin thread,
Then love must bite its tongue and turn its head.

WARWICKSHIRE, 2006

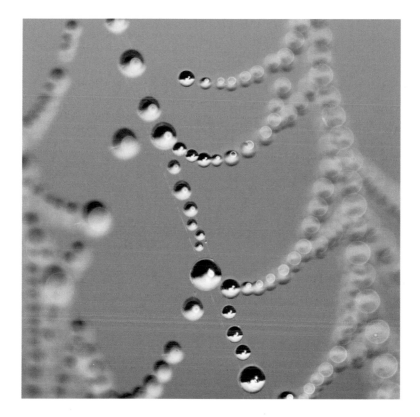

As people live longer and longer lives, the demands upon us to care for aging (and often senile) parents increases geometrically. There are many legitimate calls upon a government's purse, but our failure to sufficiently care for many such carers is a shameful indictment of our current priorities. Can we not do better in the UK and emulate the more enlightened policies practised elsewhere in Europe, especially in France? Our parents and their carers deserve no less.

Dew laden spider web.

Barnacle base.

Ranting Muses

We grow impatient waiting on your pleasure,
   Why then affect surprise when we have flown?
A muse is not some slut to take at leisure:
   You either come when called — or sleep alone.

WARWICKSHIRE, 2007

145

A decent line of poetry can come at the most inconvenient times, but poets are only human. Friends call, children interrupt, a glass of wine might clear the head. Or, more often for me: 'It's warm here in bed and the study is cold. I'll remember that line in the morning.' But mostly, you don't— and then live to regret it over the toast and marmalade.

Handstands on the Rim of Hell

A whim of birth binds mind to flesh, like brothers,
Each hybrid reads its script aloud to others,
We each know what we say, but not who plays us,
And knowing this, so each duet betrays us.

And though in times of grief or loss we ponder
This monstrous meld— yet even as we wander
Within such thickets, thorns and branches scour us,
While tigers of self-consciousness devour us.

As actors on the stage must plead and barter
With rowdies in the gods— so men must martyr
Their knowledge of the Frankenstein who plays them,
Certain that a jealous twin betrays them.

WARWICKSHIRE, 2005

Thorny oyster (Spondylus varius).

Section of Gabbro rock.

Of Mercy and Kindness

Formal mercy clothes itself in duty,
  Obnoxious to the ear and to the heart,
While kindness is itself a form of beauty,
  And all its artists masters of their art.

WARWICKSHIRE, 2005

149

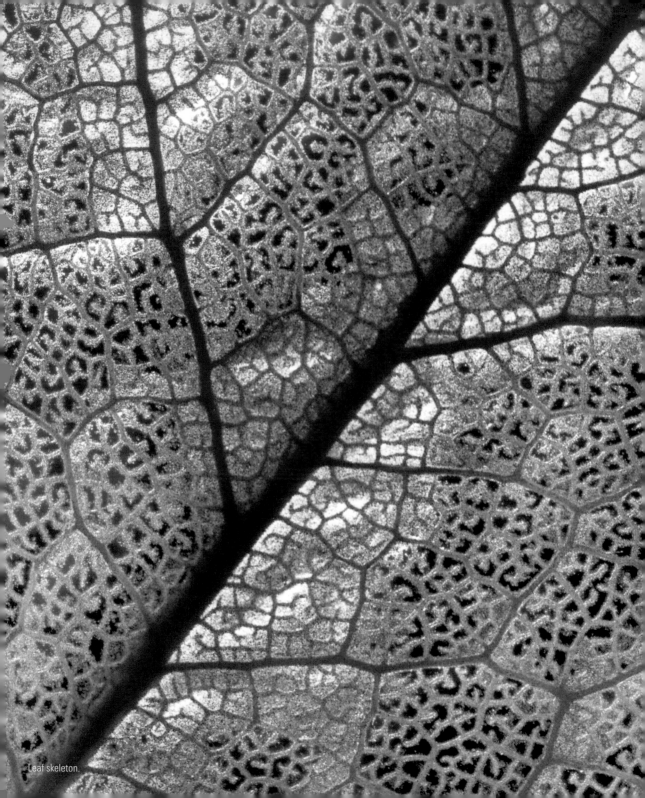

Leaf skeleton.

'We spend so long in being...'

We spend so long in being
     what we should wish to be,
Erecting and enhancing
     a thing that others see;
We keep so busy living
     as some have said we must,
Perfecting and embracing
     the sleepwalk of the just,
Concocting love and duty
     for enemies and friends,
The prisoners of a jury
     whose sentence never ends,
Too comfortable to alter
     — as exiles, we defer,
For fear we might encounter
     the ghost of who we were.

151

WARWICKSHIRE, 2007

Nero Theory

[An Alternative Theory of Human Evolution]

At long last, Nature sought to learn her span,
A question which no instinct might supply;
By hurt and trial she then selected Man
And stripped him of content: thus *'how?'* and *'why?'*
Became his only mantra— while his brain,
Too gross to force the gates of natural birth,
Ballooned within an infancy of pain
And brought him that self-knowing Men call *worth*.
Shorn bald of fur, of claw, of size or speed,
This mutant calibrator measured time
And much besides — for having slaked his need
He dwelt upon his Mother's ancient crime:
    Watch now this dragon's get pour poisoned breath
    Upon her— and, unknowing, seek her death.

WARWICKSHIRE, 2008

152

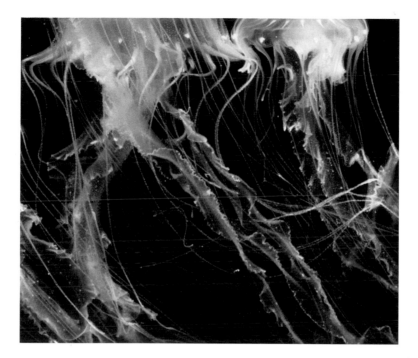

He will fail. Nature (defined as life on earth for our purpose) has survived all catastrophes for billions of years. Man's astonishingly short rise to sentiency, much of which occurred in what we call the 'Ice Age' and which defies the laws of evolutionary time spans as we currently understand them, is both a neophyte and a puny weakling in comparison. The tripling in size of an infant child's brain after birth is a unique phenomenon. (We are born with a brain just a little bigger than that of an infant gorilla.) In other words, it's a fair guess that we are merely another experiment — and perhaps one that will not be repeated. We may wipe ourselves out with our 'poisoned breath' but the dragon will barely notice our passing — unless, by some effort of will, we succeed in creating methods to transport ourselves off this planet and create colonies elsewhere. Nero, of course, was a Roman Emperor who attempted again and again to murder his odious mother, Agrippina. Collapsing ceilings and especially constructed boats (built to sink) having failed, he finally had her clubbed to death. Or so the ancients claim.

Sea nettle jellyfish (Chrysaora quinquecirrha).

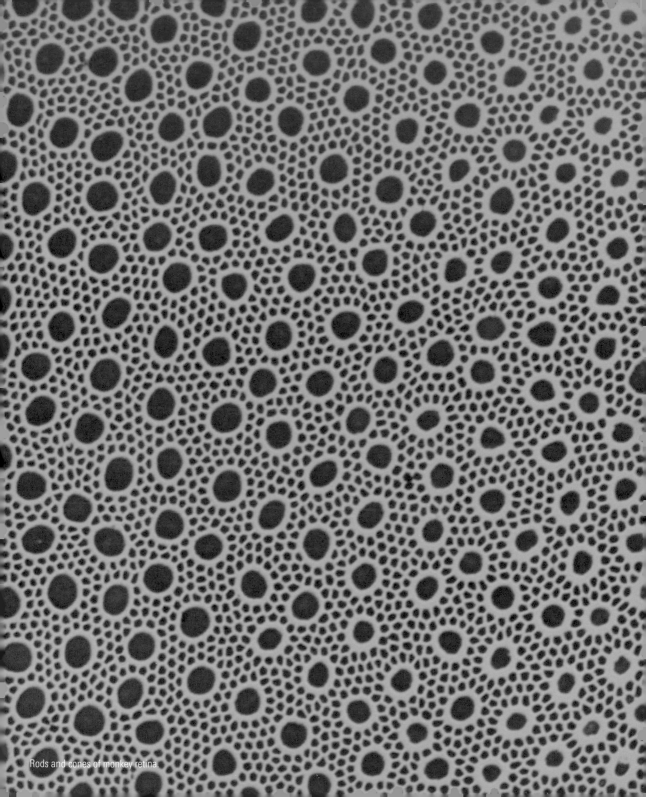
Rods and cones of monkey retina.

Wilmot to Sackville & Villiers

(While Preparing His Pet Monkey to Present at Court)

Pass round the bloody bottle, man—
It's hellish work when Lords must plan
Mere devilment for idle fools.
Sweet Jesu'— how the monster mewls.

Hold fast the mad brute's wretched arm!
I'll gut you if she comes to harm;
God damn you, Sackville, mind her teeth!
Now wrap this silken sheet beneath

Her privy parts— a pin, a pin!
Go fetch the sack and pop her in...
You ass! You fumble-fingered clown,
She's leapt, and who's to get her down?

Come friends, which peerless, noble peer
Will venture up a chandelier
To fetch my shiv'ring half-dressed ape?
Not you? 'Twas *I* who let her 'scape?

Then that's a first— proud Prince of Pox,
That John should let slip Goldilocks
When once she hath removed her clothes,
While Dorset smirks and Villiers crows.

➤

This piss-pot may not be denied,
A bowl of wine shall curb her pride—
See now, she comes —she loves to sup—
And while she swills I snap her up,

Just so! Fond limb around me curls,
We'll deck her neck in jewels and pearls,
A jade's brooch clasped to furry throat,
And French lace on her petticoat.

This turban slid upon her head—
She's fit for any sultan's bed.
The sleeping draught? 'Twas in the wine,
And when she wakes her eyes will shine.

A toast! Our merry monarch's health,
To cuckold husbands, Wit and Wealth!
To all the joy that Youth affords,
And Monkeys in the House of Lords!

WEST INDIES, 2005

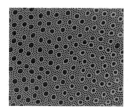

John Wilmot, 2nd Earl of Rochester, (1647-80), encompassed in his short life the roles of King's companion, abductor of women, heroic sea officer, roisterer, whoremaster, drunkard, practical joker, wit, rakehell, pornographer and Restoration poet. He died aged 33, probably of syphilis. He has been called '...one of the most remarkable and most gifted men of his remarkable and gifted century'. Rochester's poetry is not for the faint-hearted, but the best of it rings down the centuries with a moral ambivalence and intellectual honesty sadly lacking in this politically correct age. For an anodyne taste of Rochester, try any of the following poems, all widely anthologised: 'Upon Nothing', 'A Satire against Reason and Mankind', 'Rochester to the Post Boy', 'A Song of a Young Lady to an Ancient Lover' or 'The Maim'd Debauchee'. The claim that Rochester converted to Christianity during his last illness may or may not be true. What is certain is that seduction, both of reader and subject, is the cardinal virtue of his poetic works. As it was, one suspects, of his life.

Charles Sackville (6th Earl of Dorset) and George Villiers (2nd Duke of Buckingham) were Rochester's bosom companions in debauchery and high living. Rochester really did attempt to persuade Charles II to make his pet monkey a Peer of the Realm— and came perilously close to succeeding!

Karman vortices in clouds.

'Before I knew...'

Shun all astrologers, my child,
Life is leavened by surprise,
Lives foretold are lives defiled—
The eyes of innocence are wise.

And as the cruel years slow
I wish that I knew less, somehow;
To live as I lived long ago—
Before I knew what I know now.

WEST INDIES, 2008

Crystals of sucrose or saccharose.

Oven

(How Charity works for the Rich)

You may take a cake.
The cakes I bake
Are far too many— you understand?

They are free and such—
But if you touch
My oven, I'll break your goddam hand.

WEST INDIES, 2007

Butterfly wing.

In Love

All the small signs are there: the moody lurch,
   The flawless skin, bright eyes, a smile too sweet.
Yet one more giddy heart swept from its perch:
   But were hearts made to hover — or to beat?

163

WEST INDIES, 2007

Suggested by a line from the Islamic philosopher, **Ibn Hazm** (994 - 1064)

Huns mountains in south Namibia

False Messiahs

I stand with those opposed to all messiahs,
To sycophant believers — blind and deaf—
Who, if they could, would drag us through the fires
Of Faith— aye!— faith with a capital 'F'.

Always enough of new to serve their turn:
Now Christ— now Marx— now prophets long denied,
Those who would have you burn before you learn
That swastika and cross march side by side

To punish any unbelieving foe —
Star chambers pumped with gas and infidels;
Should racks prove too old-fashioned— or too slow—
Invention will provide new living hells.

Blind Faith and True Belief — twin seas to dread—
For men may drown in either, blindly led.

WARWICKSHIRE, 2006

'I talked too much...'

I talked too much—
I never learned to let a silence lie;
In company
I sought out those who spoke as loud as I.

I laughed too much—
Too long, too loud, too frequently, too plain;
I found the world
Too sad a place to celebrate its pain.

I read too much—
Too quickly, too; too wantonly, too wide;
I rarely met
A book that I could bear to cast aside.

I drank too much—
Sweet Burgundy! The glories of Bordeaux!
Come, fill a glass
And drink to absent friends who drank too slow.

I wrote too much—
This verse itself is nineteen lines too long;
And sang too much,
Yet never learned the meaning of my song.

WARWICKSHIRE, 2005

166

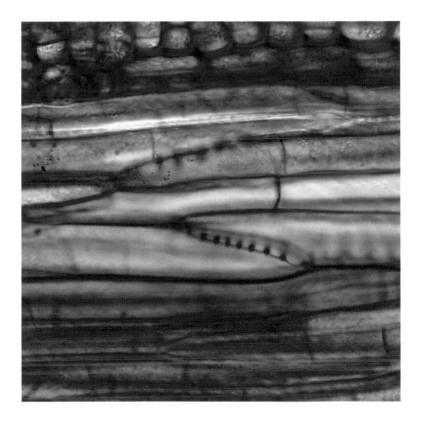

Grape vine stem.

Volcanic ice cave, Mount Erebus, Ross Island, Antarctica.

'Lover— come to me!'

Lover— come to me!
Leave the world to turn
In brute reality;
What has love to learn
Other than to flee?
Forged within the fire,
Hardened by the ice,
Exiled as pariah,
Let tenderness suffice
To licence our desire
And shame eternity.
We live the once, not twice:
Lover— come to me!

WEST INDIES, 2008

Prospero's Land

Not often— but always in flood—
  Epiphany chanced upon me:
A torrent of joy in the blood,
  A moment of ecstasy

As I fell into Prospero's land,
  Where I knew I ought not to be,
Impromptu, unbidden, unplanned—
  A veil of the world torn free,

Where Guilt had remitted his tithe
  And had married his enemy—
And Death had abandoned his scythe,
  And Time slept under a tree.

In the bantering laugh of a friend,
  Or in moments so solitary—
Though all came to grief in the end,
  Epiphany chanced upon me.

WEST INDIES, 2005

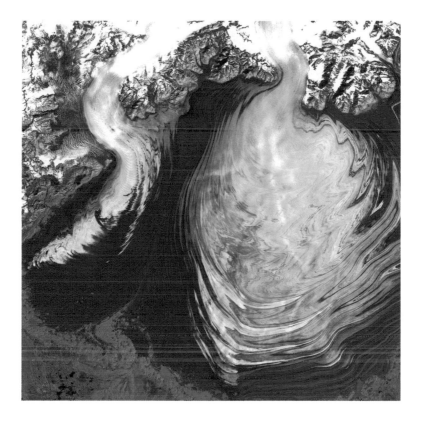

Prospero is the protagonist sorcerer on an island filled with magic in 'The Tempest', the last play Shakespeare wrote without a collaborator. Many consider Prospero's epilogue: *'Now my charms are all o'erthrown...'* to be the playwright's own 'long goodbye' to his audience.

Malaspina Glacier, Alaska.

Dry river beds, eastern Jordan.

Laying Out a Father

You laughed, and perhaps I might laugh, too,
And yet I shall hold to what is true,
Or at least to what I was taught is true,
(Which is not the same, but yet must do).

You wept, and perhaps I might have wept,
Long, long ago when innocence slept,
And a rag doll sobbed while a mother slept,
(A secret the three of us faithfully kept).

And now I must lay out a fumbling fool
Who thought to divide my legs and rule,
But what is divided makes less— as a rule,
(I was always clever at math in school).

And I lived— and memory served the lie,
But I birthed no bairn to blubber and cry,
For the lives of the lost are a heart-sick cry,
(And I would not have them suffer as I).

WEST INDIES, 2005

Sweet Lie

A hand is cupped across my breast,
His swift tongue like a hummingbird
In restless flight from flower to nest—
I know he dares not speak a word

Or cry a name, in case his cry
Betrays his heart. Instead— instead,
His mouth finds mine, his fingers fly
More fiercely now that love has fled.

His slicked back arched in ecstasy,
A sweet lie whispered through my hair—
Who is this stranger next to me?
The eyes are bright, but who is there?

WEST INDIES, 2006

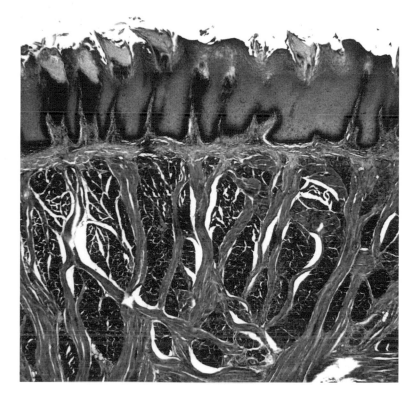

Section through human tongue.

Gullies on Mars, on a crater wall in the Newton Basin.

The Infinite Hour

Nothing is certain, nothing is sure,
   Only that death has a bloody stick;
Who can say what a life is for,
   Faith— at best— is a conjuring trick.

Nothing is certain, nothing is sure,
   Omens and oracles cloud the glass—
Cherish the infinite hour: no more;
   Fear little of what may come to pass.

Nothing is certain, nothing is sure,
   The past is a land which none defend—
Who can claim to have lived before?
   None but a fool foretells their end.

Nothing is certain, nothing is sure,
   Luck is a one-eyed queen of the blind,
Her hired assassin behind the door:
   A pox upon her— and all her kind.

Nothing is certain, nothing is sure,
   Reason is treacherous— doubt is swift,
Who can say what a life is for:
   Some cry 'punishment', some 'a gift'.

177

WEST INDIES, 2006

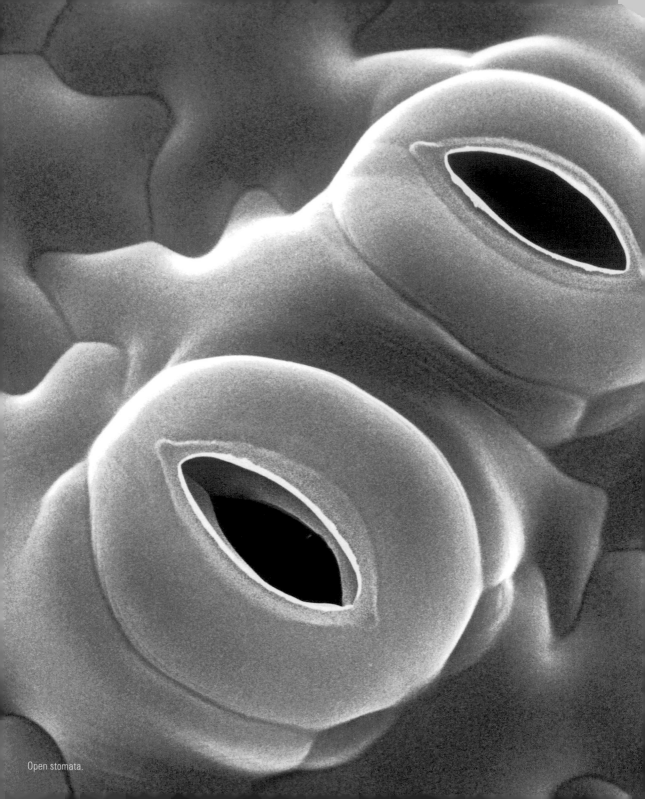

Open stomata.

Old Bailey

(Summer, 1971)

For me, there is only before
And after— after the slam
Of the Bailey's iron door,
Where the jackal lies with the lamb,

And men sit slumped in a row,
Staring or reading *The Sun*,
Where the lags and toe-rags know
What others have only begun

To accept— their guts in a knot,
Cursing and spitting and spent,
Excavating their snot—
Beginning to learn what is meant

By a 'jolt' or 'toad in the hole',
By 'Baron; or 'dint' or 'dunt',
By 'bird' or 'a nice jam roll'—
When a con from the National Front

Snarls 'Sod it!', his eyes like slits,
And the cage is suddenly hot
As he turns: 'I see these poncey gits...'
He nods, (eyes slide to us), 'have got

Just what they fuckin' deserve.
One thing I hate,' his voice beer flat,
'Is bunkin' with a bleeding perv'
Who messes with kiddies an' that.'

➤

And the room grows stiller than ice,
And my face is a mask of snow,
When a drowsy Irish voice
Purrs: 'What would an arse'ole know

But what he reads in the news,
(Which I learned to read in school)
Or the lies we're fed by screws?
And these ain't pervs, you fool,

Read this!' And he folds the rag
And slides it across the floor
And winks while I hand him a fag.
For me, there is only before...

And after— after the raid,
Where coppers as bent as a hinge
March in and bellow their trade:
'We've come for the drugs and minge!

'This is the Dirty Squad!
Stand up when I'm talking to you!
You're in fer it now, by God!
If only you bleeders knew!'

And ten of 'em, count 'em, *ten*,
Of Her Majesty's Scotland Yard,
Red-nosed and warranted men
Who think themselves 'well 'ard',

Harder than coffin nails,
As hard as Desperate Dan,
Bundle our office files in bales
And lug them out to a van,

And call the secretaries sluts,
And help themselves to tea,
And use our phone, no ifs or buts,
And turn to Kenny and me,

And warn us, there and then,
That 'a nudge is as good as a wink
To a blind horse, *g-e-n-t-l-e-m-e-n*,'
As they toss the cups in the sink,

And trash the coats on the rack,
And force the lock in a drawer,
And vanish, yelling 'We'll be back!'
For me, there is only before...

And after— after we learned
What I guess we already knew,
That as far as the law is concerned,
There is no such thing as 'true'

Or 'false'— there is only 'the norm',
And the stick-brittle words of a judge
With his 'duty to perform',
(Serving a politician's grudge),

➤

With his wig and his worldly squint,
Spouting his sanctimonious bile,
Happy to see his face in print,
Smiling his dry-lipped crocodile smile,

Explaining away, with shop-worn mirth,
To twelve good men and true,
Just what 'the evidence' is worth
Of a man like me or you,

As he bends and buckles to fit
Some Cinderella's pump
On an elephant's foot, the crafty git,
And gives the bench a thump

As he waffles and witters away,
Hinting between the lines
That a judge knows more than he can say
(Or cares to share with Philistines)

But he knows when 'a thing is lewd!'
And brings himself up short,
Then sends the jury out to brood
And toddles off for his port...

While lawyers we can't afford
Caw like a murder of crows
That 'his Lordship's summing-up was flawed,
But that's the way it goes...

Most helpful on Appeal...
Quite frankly, a disgrace...'
And leave us to toy with our meal
Knowing we'd lost the case.

For me, there is only before
And after— after the slam
Of the Bailey's iron door,
Where the jackal lies with the lamb,

Where the lags can make you a cutter
With fags and matches and soap,
And trusties shuffle and mutter,
(One with a telescope

Concealed in his wooden legs).
Where screws are as thick as a plank,
And the cries of a man as he begs
While they cut his balls with a shank

Are drowned in the clatter and roar
Of piss-filled buckets and pails—
Carried from each cell door
To a place where all hope fails,

Where men are buggered and reamed,
Their bodies bruised and numb,
And those who scuff are double-teamed
While playing deaf and dumb,

➤

Where a squealer finds ground glass
Has sweetened his morning brew,
'Now shut your effin' mouth, you arse,
There's nuffink you c'n do.'

And nor there is— you understand?
Not in the bowels of the law,
Not in the jails of this fair land.
For me, there is only before

And after— after the key
Had turned on a sliver of doubt,
As word came down from the powers that be
To let the buggers out.

And a Law Lord let us go,
And the free air tasted sweet,
But there wasn't man who didn't know
He spoke for Downing Street.

And I swore myself an oath
That if wealth and clout would serve,
Then I should apply myself to both,
To hold them in reserve

In a world where the rules are clear:
That only the rich have wings,
And the one beast all such bastards fear
Is coin, and the power it brings.

BEGUN: WARWICKSHIRE, 2004
COMPLETED: WEST INDIES, 2007

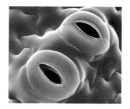

OZ was a 'counter-culture' magazine of the late 1960's and early 1970's. Originally founded in Australia, it was launched in London in 1967 by Richard Neville. I joined the magazine in 1968. Then came Ted Heath's government in 1970. The OZ offices were raided again and again by Scotland Yard's so-called 'Dirty Squad', officially the Obscene Publications Division of the Metropolitan Police. Eventually they charged three OZ editors, Richard, Jim Anderson and me, with a serious crime, using an archaic law: Conspiracy to Pervert the Morals of the Young of the Realm. This led to the longest conspiracy trial in British history. We eventually beat the 'conspiracy' rap but were sent to prison for two minor charges tacked on as an afterthought. The public outcry was so great we were swiftly released (highly unusually, it should be noted) prior to our successful appeal and after serving time in Wormwood Scrubs and Wandsworth prisons. Later, the 'Dirty Squad' was discovered to be institutionally corrupt and many of its officers were sent to prison and the squad disbanded. It emerged they had targeted OZ because they were taking so many bribes from pornographers they suffered from a poor arrest record. The 1970's today seem as remote as the Middle Ages, but I would make three points: When you hear the word 'conspiracy' in a court of law, you can be almost certain there is monkey-business afoot. Secondly, prisons in Britain are overcrowded because we imprison more of our citizens than all but a few countries in the world. Many of these prisoners are mentally ill. Lastly, the judiciary in Britain is deeply flawed. More than one senior barrister refused, against their sworn oath, to represent OZ, probably because they felt that to do so might harm their career. (We were fortunate that John Mortimer accepted our case.) Our own trial judge was so eager to convict us that his summing up has become a byword for incompetence and bias. And the judiciary's political masters, including the Home Secretary and others, were involved in the whole shabby episode up to their wattled necks. No system of law can be perfect and I have heard it argued that much has changed for the better, judicially speaking, in recent years in Britain. Maybe. But I doubt it. I very, very much doubt it.

'With weakness comes...'

With weakness comes the force that fuses breath
To need. Perfection shrinks within its mind,
And knowing this, then seeks the perfect death,
Which is itself a weakness— of a kind.

The needs that drive us spring from discontent—
Thus I arose this morning filled with fire,
Though who can say which part was nature's bent
And which the sinking ashes of desire?

Forgive me, Bodhisattva — yet who grew
The wheat that made the cakes these pilgrims bring
To set outside your cave? Are they all, too,
The broken reeds of which your gospels sing?

This only I will grant: in weakness lies
The need permitting charlatans to rise.

WARWICKSHIRE, 2008

Maharishi Mahesh Yogi, guru and tycoon, died on February 5th, 2008 aged 91. 'Mahesh' was a part of his original name; the rest was invented. In 1998 his organisation boasted a property portfolio worth $3 billion. He made his name on the back of The Beatles and spent the rest of his life denying it, dying in a closely-guarded Dutch wooden fortress, a world hosting its own ministers, laws and currency, a fantasy land where opulence and luxury meet Vedic Mantras and where deluded saps paid massive sums to heal their souls. Let John Lennon have the last word. When The Beatles stormed out of his Indian ashram after the Maharishi (which means 'perfect soul') made a pass at Mia Farrow in 1968, the guru asked why they were leaving. 'If your so fucking cosmic, you'll know!' answered Lennon, and proceeded to write the song 'Sexy Sadie' (originally called 'Maharishi'). The song's best line is: 'You made a fool of everyone'. Aye, that he did, John. That he did.

Lenticular cloud.

Agate surface.

'Sunset, mid-July...'

Sunset, mid-July— the failing light
Salutes a sway-backed cedar on the lawn
And liquefies the words I thought to write:
Not all nights are followed by a dawn,

And not all hurts can ever be put right.
The glory of the world, which sick men mourn
As life leaks out of them, remains as bright
As on the very day that they were born.

Harvested or not, the ripening corn
Will grow— the moon will rise due east tonight.
Not all nights are followed by a dawn,
And not all hurts can ever be put right.

WARWICKSHIRE, 2006

This is the Song

This is the song that none can sing,
This is the gift the old gods bring,
Sung this once as the soul takes wing
In the emptiness of night.

Here is the powerlessness of speech,
The letting go that none can teach,
The song of things beyond our reach
Singing to its own light.

WEST INDIES, 2007

Kingfisher wing feathers (Alcedo atthis).

November 1915

(Albert Einstein muses in his Berlin apartment)

The Frankensteins of light and matter waltz
To choreographies of the sublime,
While gravity sweeps partners, true and false,
Into the arms of non-existent time.

So ether dies, and half of what was taught
By Newton's worshippers now lies undone—
Their sacrament a martyr to a thought:
All space, all time, all matter— all are one.

Should I prove mad, what certainties are lost?
My murders neither blight the stars or mud;
While madmen smash a world at any cost
The trench of Newton's coffin leaks no blood.

Dear Isaac: I must check my math once more—
And then dispatch my troops to slay your Law.

WARWICKSHIRE, 2007

Backbone running across the Milky Way.

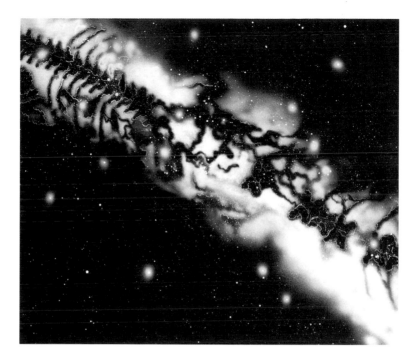

As the hell of World War I erupted around him, Albert Einstein, an outspoken pacifist, finally resolved the difficulties inherent in his 1905 Special Theory of Relativity and came at last to his Holy Grail, the General Theory of Relativity. It is fashionable to denigrate Einstein today in some quarters, due to his later doubts concerning the 'reality' of a beast he helped birth himself— quantum theory. Be that as it may, in the words of one contemporary: "...the General Theory of Relativity changed the intellectual and scientific landscape as nothing has, or perhaps ever will, again." It was a work of genius, made even more poignant by Einstein's reverence for Isaac Newton, whose iron laws governing a mechanical universe were shattered by both the Special and General Theories. Newton's portrait hung in Einstein's study until the day he died. 'Ether' was a substance scientists had claimed must exist for centuries— a kind of invisible, unmeasurable 'soup' in which everything, including light and other forms of electromagnetic radiation, 'floated'. One of Einstein's insights was that ether was little more than a collective figment of the scientific establishment's imagination. The best biography of Einstein I know is *Einstein: His Life and Universe* by Walter Isaacson (Simon & Schuster, 2007). I have read it twice: once for the pure enjoyment of its prose style and storytelling and subsequently to help me come to grips with the science of 20th-century physics. A terrific book, recommended for anyone with an interest in the world and universe around us.

'I have the talent, sometimes...'

I have the talent, sometimes, not to care:
To leap while others think,
To glance when others blink,
To stare into the brink and not to fall:
There is no merit in it — but it's there.

I have the talent, sometimes, to be wrong:
To shrug and walk away,
To cauterise the day,
To hear, but not obey the sirens' call.
(And in the weaker places to be strong.)

I have the talent, sometimes, from afar,
To see what might be done,
To turn as others run,
To stop and shoulder one too weak to crawl:
There is no merit being — what you are.

WEST INDIES, 2006

Eroded rock beds near the Layla Oasis in the Arabian desert, Saudi Arabia.

Much Too Much

The problem with much too much
Is not its inventory,
Not what you take or what you touch,
But what it seeks to be.

The problem with much too much
Is that it's simply that,
Its width replaces depth to such
Degree, the world grows flat.

The problem with much too much
Lies in its freight of dross
Which skews the mind to form a crutch,
Imagining its loss.

WARWICKSHIRE, 2006

Human fingerprint.

You Cannot Understand

Look, you could never understand,
So don't go on and on,
There's a good chap; at second-hand
Each duckling is a swan,
Like mourners with their eulogies
Who mean well, by their lights,
But seeking far too hard to please,
Please no one.
      How the nights
Are drawing in— I'll light the fire
And pour us both a glass,
But only if you don't admire
Or seek to turn to farce
What farce itself is powerless
To smooth, at least to me:
It's not so much the senselessness
It's... Christ just let it be!
Let's talk of beer, or famous men,
The rest leaves me unmanned,
We'll come to it, though God knows when:
You cannot understand.

WEST INDIES, 2007

A maelstrom of embers whips across a field near Santa Clarita, California. Driven by Santa Anas.

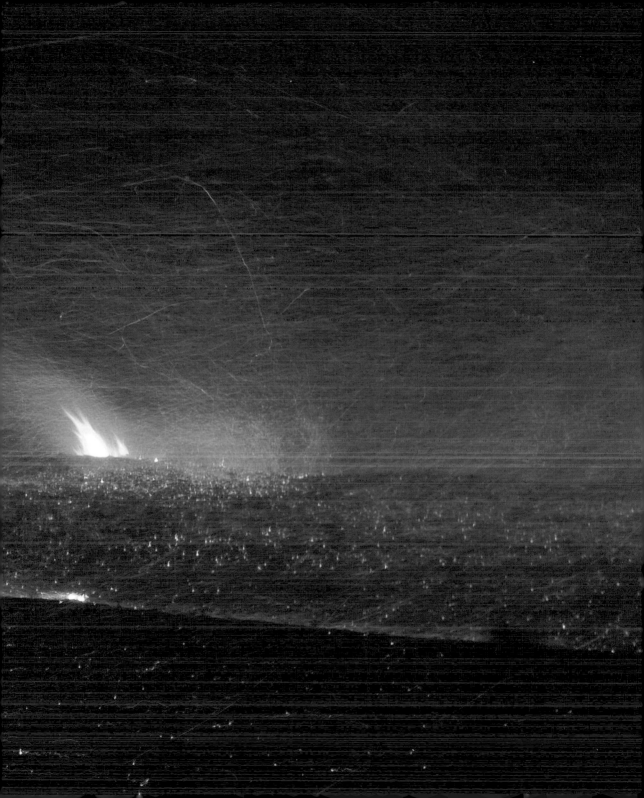

Circular deposits in Spotted Lake, British Columbia, Canada.

'I plucked all the cherries...'

I plucked all the cherries
Chance would allow,
Take them, and welcome—
I'm done with them now.

Done with the ladder
And done with the tree,
Take them, and welcome—
They're no use to me.

Done with the getting of
What I could get,
Take it, and welcome—
Try not to forget

To pluck all the cherries
Chance will allow,
Take them, and welcome—
I'm done with them now.

WEST INDIES, 2006

Addiction

I can't.
You can't? We both know what we need.
I CAN'T!
You see? The tiger needs to feed.

I won't.
You will... we both know how it stands.
I WON'T!
Why not? There's no one understands.

Get out.
To where? I live inside your head.
Get OUT!
No dice. I'll sleep when I've been fed.

Shut up.
I have. That's you you're listening to.
Shut UP!
Oh boy. Just wake me when you're through.

Not now.
Uh huh. We've been through this before.
NOT NOW!
Uh huh. The stuff is in the drawer.

It hurts.
Of course. The biter's being bit.
It HURTS!
Me too. Now get us both a hit.

Just one.
Yeah, sure— one goddam motherlode.
Just ONE!
Just one. And one more for the road.

No one can understand addiction who has not been addicted. Turning addicts into criminals, ostensibly to keep others from coming into contact with addictive substances, may seem like good sense. But it's not. Truly it's not. All political and legal wars on drugs are self-defeating. Ask any senior policeman — in confidence after a couple of glasses of wine. Many will tell you that drugs should be legalized and strictly controlled and that addiction should be treated as a medical, not a legal issue, just as we did in earlier times, very successfully. Demonizing addicts and drug abuse may make us feel better, but can anyone deny that such a policy has failed us all dismally? Perhaps it is time to think the unthinkable.

Valve in a human heart's left ventricle.

Patterns in sheet ice on a river.

Quite Soon

Quite soon, the world will turn without me here:
And then? The stars will shine, the moon will rise,
And in a wood the wolves will stalk a deer.

The young will clock off work and sip their beer
And speak of those they worship or despise.
So soon, the world will turn without me here

While crowds at cricket matches clap and cheer,
And, top of class, a shy girl takes her prize.
Within a wood the wolves will stalk a deer

As anglers fling their floats beside a weir,
And backstage, some young Portia dabs her eyes.
Too soon, the world will turn without me here

While 'auld lang syne' rings out another year,
And, in a house close by, an infant cries,
And in a wood, far off, wolves stalk a deer.

Though men may ply among the stars and peer
Upon strange suns, or - stranger still! - grow wise,
Quite soon, the world will turn without me here:
And in a wood the wolves will stalk a deer.

WEST INDIES, 2006

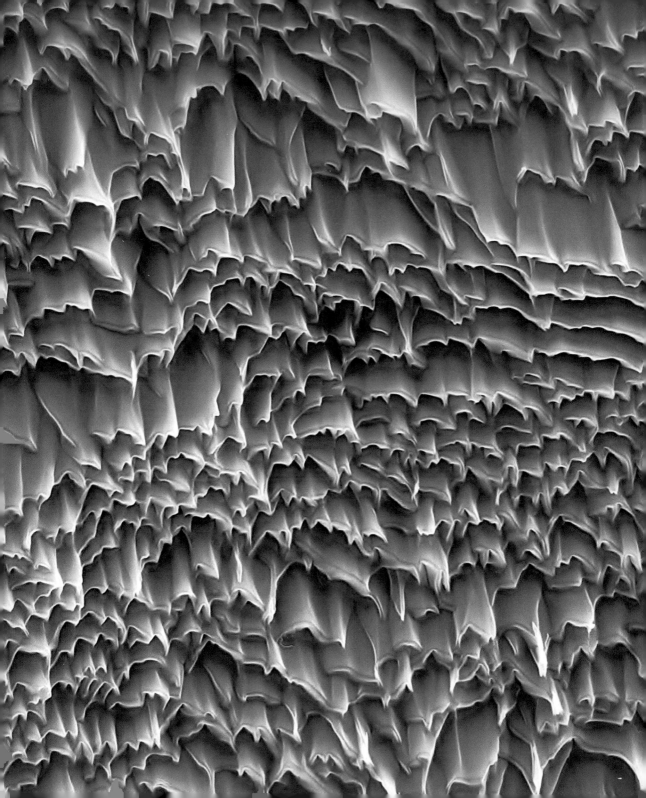

You're Wrong (Tough Love)

You're wrong. It's not your mother or your father,
No matter what you say, my dear. It's you.
The long words of the clever ones— or rather,
The ones who named the demons that you slew —
Are bunk. And while I'm at it, I shall mention
That what they are— are crocodiles in tears,
Their clever-dick asides are condescension,
As if your will was governed by the spheres.
The tattoos you have pricked upon your knuckles,
Those rings you have inserted for applause,
That innocent who wriggles while he suckles
Your swollen breast— are symptoms, not a cause.
  The State's caress will slam your future shut:
  Nor are you such men's burden, or their slut.

WARWICKSHIRE, 2006

Thoth's Gift

(The god Ammon remonstrates with Thoth following the latter's gift of the written word to Mankind)

I see they scratch on stone and bark
To tally days and years,
While slyer scribes now make their mark
To tabulate their fears.

A princely gift— and kindly meant—
Yet we may rue the day
You shewed them... this... impediment...
And led such minds astray.

The songs of old, of blood and wrath,
Of love and war now lie
Cold captive — I foretell you, Thoth,
This gift shall see gods die.

These 'alphabets' but grant them leave
In learning— to forget;
Nor shall their children's children grieve
For Ammon, Thoth or Set.

WEST INDIES, 2004

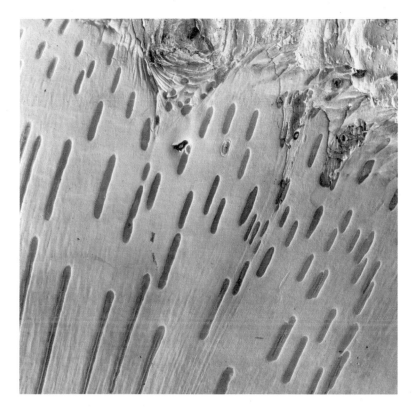

A story told by Socrates in Plato's *Phaedrus*. Ammon (the Greek form of Amen-ra) was the King of Egyptian gods. Thoth was the lunar god, master of annals, law and hieroglyphs. Set (or Seth) was a god considered the incarnation of evil, having murdered his brother, Osiris. And, indeed, Ammon was right. The collective memory of mankind encapsulated by writing, led, after many centuries, to the Enlightenment— which, though forgotten by many today, still shines like a beacon in Western philosophy, urging mankind to renounce the cruelty, hatreds and endless wars which have been the one unremitting inheritance of organised religion. Thank you, Thoth. Thank you. (Although I know you never existed!)

Monarch birch trunk.

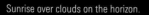
Sunrise over clouds on the horizon.

True Love

True love shoulders any weight,
   Soldiering in secret mazes,
Shreds the wire and scales the gate,
   Blind to disapproving gazes.
Shut out— true love battles through.
(And if it fail, it was not true.)

True love's warrant knows no border,
   Forging visas, bribing guards,
Feral, like some crazed marauder
   Practising absurd charades.
Thwarted— true love turns the screw.
(And if it fail, it was not true.)

True love shames the rising sun
   Laughing at its feeble heat;
In that glare, strange deeds are done,
   Love knows nothing of defeat.
Banished— true love plots anew.
(And if it fail, it was not true.)

WEST INDIES, 2008

'You're bored, child?'

Look at the birds.
Learn to listen to their chatter,
Their flitting, twittering flights for no
Discernible purpose; the clatter
And the cawing of that black crow,
The furtive, dry-leaved peck and scrape
Of blackbirds blundering in a bush
Seeking worms and beetles; the shape
Of the wagtail's wing; the shove and push
Of tits among the bacon rinds;
The eerie, invisible knock,
Knock knock as a woodpecker finds
A bark grub; the wheeling starling flock.
Look at the birds.

Look at the earth.
Scoop up a handful in your palm.
Not for nothing have men plundered,
Murdered, fought and wrought great harm
Among their kind — whole empires sundered —
Just to own it, or to believe
They did. Crumble it. What's it worth?
Ask a farmer stooping to sheave
A field of sun ripe wheat. The Earth!
The land! Listen, listen to me!
The blood of kings lies in your hand,
What came before— and what shall be.
Think on it. Seek to understand.
Look at the earth.

Altocumulus clouds forming a mackerel sky.

Look at the sky.
An emptiness? The blue-walled womb
Of all that is, of all that ever
Grazed or grew or swam —and met its doom —
Beneath our tyrant sun. Forever
Heaving, blowing, sleeting, snowing,
Raining, resting — bringing with the night
Its velvet, eerie canvas, glowing
With long dead messengers of light.
And yet, who looks — with wit to see?
Should you take long enough to chart
This wheel of time and mystery
Life's miracle will swamp your heart.
Look at the sky.

You're *bored*, child?

'I am listening, now...'

I am listening, now. The past is past,
I'm here. I'm sitting beside your bed.
Speak to me now. It's time at last
To make amends. The past is dead.

I am listening, now. I'm here, my dear.
Your spotted hands are soft as fur.
Speak to me, now. I've ears to hear,
They are not so deaf as once they were.

I am listening, now. I'm done with fuss;
Babble of treachery, love or pain,
Speak of yourself, of them, of us—
Speak of the ghosts that fill the rain.

I am listening, now. I left it late,
Later than ever we thought or knew.
Speak to me. Please. Unbar the gate.
Turn back, my dear. I'm here for you.

WEST INDIES, 2005

'...but the rain is full of ghosts tonight...'
— **Edna St. Vincent Millay**

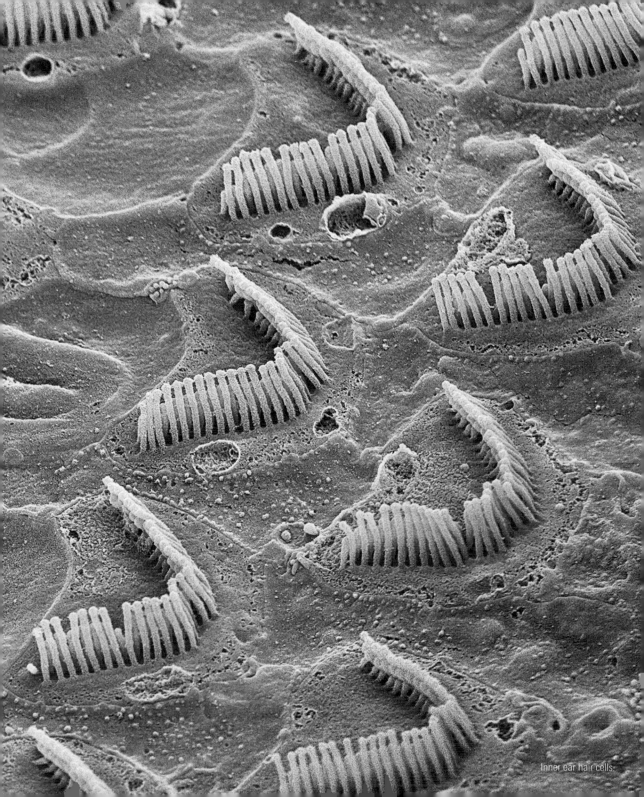

Inner ear hair cells.

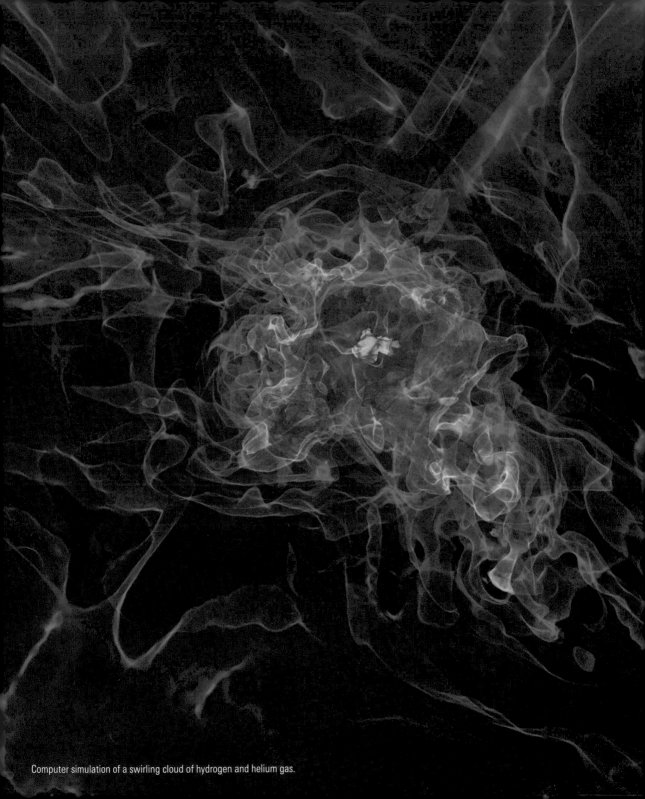

Computer simulation of a swirling cloud of hydrogen and helium gas.

The Cup of War

For those who fight, the cup of war
Is neither right nor wrong,
Each brew too pale, too long in store—
Too bitter or too strong.

Back home the nodding donkeys dare
To spout what soldiers think,
But soldiers neither know nor care—
The order comes, you drink!

The squaddies sworn to drain its dregs
Pay no respect to shame,
Their missing arms and missing legs
Will bleed or rot the same.

Their masters bless the stinking cup
And fill it to the brink,
They've not the balls to suck it up—
The order comes: *you drink!*

WARWICKSHIRE, 2007

False fire urchin (Astropyga radiata).

'Not all things go wrong...'

Not all things go wrong, and knowing
This, be wary of despair,
As you go through hell — keep going,
Make no brave oasis there.

Through the shadowlands of grieving,
Past the giants, Doubt and Fear,
Heartsick, stunned, and half believing —
Heed no whisper in your ear.

Not all things go wrong — and after
Winter's famine comes the spring,
Kindness, beauty, children's laughter —
Joy is ever on the wing.

WEST INDIES, 2008

A Note on the Poems

In response to questions I'm often asked at poetry readings, I offer the following *apologia*. Readers may wish to bear in mind Christopher Morley's definition of poets as 'those with the courage to leave ajar the door to madness'.

I began writing poetry, completely unexpectedly, in September 1999 while recovering from an illness. I attempt to write for at least three hours a day on the basis of Mark Twain's dictum that 'most inspiration comes from the application of the seat of the pants to the seat of the chair'. A Fleet Street journalist has observed that I write 'like a man obsessed': perhaps I am subconsciously attempting to make up for lost time? I constantly make notes, having discovered that if a promising line or subject arrives in my head, it is necessary for me to reduce it to writing immediately – delay can be fatal to its recovery.

Sometimes I write poetry directly onto one of my computers. There are eleven of these elderly dinosaurs scattered about the world in various summerhouses, cottages, offices, apartments, barns and bolt-holes. There does not appear to be any difference, for me at least, in the quality of poems created on a computer compared with those begun on paper. All my poems (1,101 of them as I write) are stored in a primitive database. When I'm done with a poem, I squirrel it away and try not refer to it for a year or two, revising only to make selections for a new book or when preparing for a poetry tour. I try to keep in mind the wry observation of an earlier poet who said that no poem is ever really 'completed'; it is merely abandoned by its author.

At other times, I get stuck. Either I cannot write anything worthwhile or I suspect that the form or meter I am wrestling with has usurped the poem's original *raison d'être*. Should this occur, I force myself to abandon the blighter and bang it into a folder marked 'Poems In Progress'. In the early days I tended to soldier on, which often led to second-rate work. Other writers have helped me to come to understand that structure is merely a vessel, not the wine, and that spoiled wine in a fancy decanter is vinegar by any other name. Nor is the degree of my absorption in any piece of writing a true guide. A bad poem, or one merely strong in the weak places, is still a bad poem, no matter what the cost in labour of its birth pains. Some of my best poems arrive effortlessly; others are the result of months of blood, sweat and tears. There appears to be (forgive the pun) no rhyme or reason to it.

Audience reaction plays a part in the selection of poems for a new book. While no single audience is infallible, their sustained, collective view is very nearly so, in my experience. An extensive selection of my poetry, written and recorded, can be found on **www.felixdennis.com** including some yet to be published in book form. Visitors to the site are encouraged to leave any comments they may wish to make.

Possibly because I write in traditional forms loathed by the druids-in-residence of modern poetry and perhaps because I no longer starve in a garret, my coming-out as a poet was greeted with venomous derision by one or two of Grub Street's more rarefied flowers. I fared better elsewhere: Michael Boyd, Creative Director of the RSC; the late Robert Woof at the Wordsworth Trust; presenter and author, Melvyn Bragg and US novelist and critic, Tom Wolfe, all encouraged me to continue. I am very, very grateful to them. Early encouragement from the right quarter is a priceless gift.

My advice to aspiring poets, then, is: keep writing, listen to constructive criticism and ignore the rest. Try, too, to find an editor you trust and respect. Difficult, I know: the likes of Simon Rae do not grow on trees. And buy yourself a copy of Stephen Fry's 'The Ode Less Travelled'– easily the most humane, witty and helpful book on prosody in print.

A question I am frequently confronted with concerns intent. Do I write poetry to be performed, to be recorded, or to sit quietly on the page? As anyone familiar with the subject will confirm, some of our finest poets are, or were, very poor readers of their own work. (To test this, visit the wonderful website created by Richard Carrington and Andrew Motion, **www.poetryarchive.org** which features, alongside much else, historical recordings by outstanding poets.) Even so, poetry, in essence, is an oral art, a form of song older by far than written prose. Rhyme and meter developed partly as a mnemonic device, enabling elders to instruct as well as to entertain tribal members for countless generations– long, long before the first hieroglyphs were scratched on rock or bark. (See 'Thoth's Gift' on page 208.)

The answer, then, is that I write poetry to be read aloud while knowing that most readers, indeed, the majority of readers, will not follow suit; knowing, too, that only a small percentage will ever attend one of my readings. Instead, my publishers include a free audio CD with my books. Having heard actors from the Royal Shakespeare Company reading my poetry on stage, I am aware that I have neither the talent nor training to match them. Even so, working with George Taylor and Dan Gable, I sit in a studio three or four times a year recording most poems I write. These recordings appear in the audio CDs found in my books, on my own website and others, on the special audio books created by libraries for the blind and on radio programmes like BBC Radio 4's 'Poetry Please'.

Does it all matter? Three years ago a woman came up to me after a poetry reading. She was crying softly. As I signed her book, she kept saying: 'How could you know? How could you know? You are not a mother. How could you know?' She squeezed my shoulder as her husband led her away into the night.

So, yes. It bloody well *does* matter– to me and to her, at least.

While it is idle for authors to feign total indifference to applause or brickbats, as any history of literary criticism will show, all in all, I am convinced that I write mainly for myself. I know that I would continue to write verse if no other soul in the world expressed interest. I write to discover who I am, to escape the carapace inherited from a life spent earning filthy lucre, to stave off a predilection for other addictions and, primarily, to experience the sheer joy of weaving words to shape ideas. As a somewhat noisome beast, perhaps I should have inflicted my verse making onto an unsuspecting world anonymously, using a *nom de plume*. (This was the very advice I received from well-meaning friends.) But to have done so would have deprived me of the pleasure of performing my work in public.

I can recall the astonishment and barely concealed glee at the announcement my first British poetry reading in London's West End. *'He's doing what? Lord, oh Lord what an ass! We have to go. It should be hilarious.'* And it is true that the room was packed to gills with salivating non-believers. Coming out as a poet is not for the faint of heart. Poetry in the modern world is not for wimps.

But just as the levels of concentration and time required are scarcely comprehensible to the uninitiated, so, too, are the rewards. The warm glow of satisfaction when an obdurate stanza shyly emerges after hours spent pummeling it in mumbling silence is matched only by the adrenaline rush and exhilaration of catching an audience by the throat with it months later. The making of money can be absorbing, fun even; but it cannot hold a candle to the risk / reward ratio involved in writing and performing.

As Lord Chesterton remarked: 'It is hell to write but heaven to have written.' Amen to that, would say most writers. Why, then, do we continue to descend into the depths of Chesterton's hell? For some, like Dr. Johnson, the answer might be 'to make a living': (not that I believe him for a minute). For others, 'to make a reputation' or simply, 'because I can'.

For me, it is the result of a chance discovery made nine years ago in a hospital bed: that the flame of poetry cauterizes the wound of life as nothing else can.

226

Acknowledgements

Homeless in My Heart has been long in gestation and I wish to thank Caroline Rush who oversaw each stage of its production. Ian Leggett engineered the resurrection of Britain's finest colour printer, Butler & Tanner, who have printed it so splendidly. George Taylor and Dan Gable recorded and produced the accompanying audio CD with their usual combination of amused efficiency and creative savvy. Mick Watson's Class Act team continue to ensure that my poetry readings are at least technical *tours de force* while Fiona MacIntyre and her colleagues at Ebury Press somehow sell far more copies of my books of verse that I deserve. Elena Chiesa in Rome has produced four stunning video animations of my poems for public viewing and I hope will be persuaded to create many more. Sarah Locke of Braben & Co, despite years of patient effort, has yet to train me in the art of keeping my big mouth shut; fortunately, her media skills smooth over the majority of my public pratfalls. When on the road touring, Toby Fisher, Wendy Kasabian, Ashleigh Clarke, Steven Kotok, Thom Stretton, Julian Guy, Mervyn Hudman, Fiona Lindsay and a cast of what seems like thousands play their heroic parts while the likes of Rebecca Ho, Michael Hyman, David Bliss, Cathy Galt and Don Sheppard keep the home fires burning. And let us not forget the Gulfstream jet and helicopter pilots, for all love; I forget all their names, but they know very well who they are. The wonderful mystery writer, John Lawton, (do try his Inspector Troy novels — the best combination of literature and suspense since le Carré), unwittingly supplied the title of this book with a throwaway line delivered in the midst of the London Blitz. My editor, Simon Rae and reader, Moni Mannings were as invaluable as ever — I should be lost without them. Using arcane arts unknown to ordinary mortals, the online staff at Dennis Publishing under Peter Wootton keep my gargantuan poetry website **www.felixdennis.com** humming. I am especially indebted to designer Rebecca Jezzard, whose work speaks for itself, to Bill Sanderson and Mikki Rain for their illustrations and to Science Photo Library and The National Geographic archives for *Homeless in My Heart's* stupendous, if occasionally chilling, photography. Lastly, as always, I thank the companion of my heart, Marie-France, together with the many friends I have cheerfully abused as guinea-pigs while auditioning these poems around numerous dining room tables and over countless bottles of wine.

Index